PILGRIMAGE

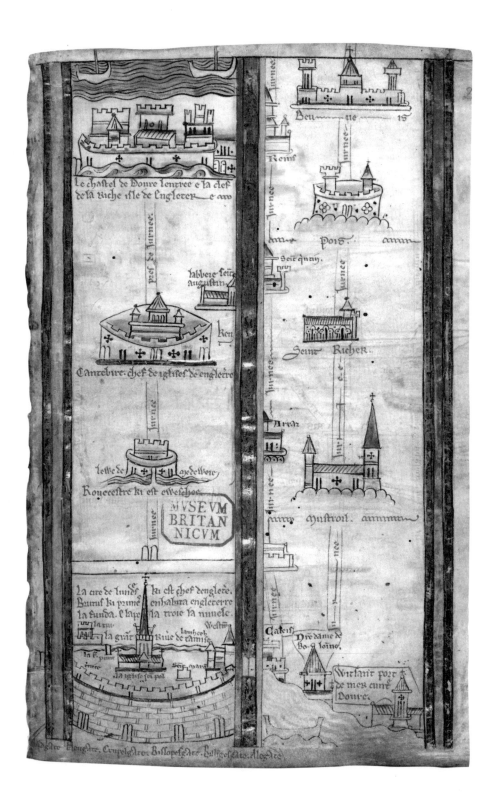

Le chastel de Donre lentree e la clef
de la riche isle de Engleter   e aw

pref de Jurnee.

labbeie seie
Augustin

Ken

Cantebure: chef deglises de engletere

Jurnee

lesse de   lage de More
Rouecestre ki est eweschee:

Jurnee

MVSEVM
BRITAN
NICVM

Jurnee

La cire de lundes ki est chef denglede.
Burus ki prime enhabita engleterre
la funda. l'apela la troie la nuuele
                              Westm
            lambech
la grat   Riue de tamise
la E prim
enne   Seir mara
      la iglese sei pol.

Jurnee

Beu   ue   15

Rens

Jurnee

Jurnee

Pois

Seir equny.

Jurnee

Seint Richer.

Arudz

Jurnee

Chustroil.

nee

Jurnee

Cadeis

Nre dame de
Bo loine.

Wiclaiuportt
de mer cunt
Donre.

PILGRIMAGE

JOURNEYS OF MEANING

PETER STANFORD

With 26 illustrations

To Kit – *the best of pilgrimage companions*

Frontispiece: Section of an illustrated itinerary from London to Jerusalem, by Matthew Paris, 1250–59

First published in the United Kingdom in 2021 by Thames & Hudson Ltd, 181A High Holborn, London WC1V 7QX

First published in the United States of America in 2021 by Thames & Hudson Inc., 500 Fifth Avenue, New York, New York 10110

Pilgrimage: Journeys of Meaning
© 2021 Thames & Hudson Ltd, London
Text © 2021 Peter Stanford

Typeset by Mark Bracey

British Library Cataloguing-in-Publication Data
A catalogue record for this book is available from the British Library

Library of Congress Control Number 2020940730

ISBN 978-0-500-25241-3

Printed and bound in India by Replika Press Pvt. Ltd

Alander Avensis.

CONTENTS

THE NEW GEOGRAPHY OF SPIRITUAL POWER

※

'For in their hearts doth Nature stir them so,
Then people long on pilgrimage to go,
And palmers to be seeking foreign strands,
To distant shrines renowned in sundry lands.'

GEOFFREY CHAUCER,
THE CANTERBURY TALES (C. 1387–1400)

My initiation into the time-honoured religious ritual of pilgrimage came as a naive 17-year-old. A group of us from my Catholic school in Liverpool travelled to Lourdes in France. We had all grown up being told about how, since 1858, when the Virgin Mary had appeared there to the young Bernadette Soubirous, this shrine had been an otherworldly place, linked by an invisible thread to heaven. Spiritual and even physical illnesses could be cured by bathing in the waters that Jesus' mother had caused to gush into a grotto.

Though in my narrow, traditional Catholic world of the time I didn't know it, I was also stepping out on that journey in the

7

footsteps of millions of pilgrims down the ages who have headed off in the search for meaning along well-trodden paths to holy spots around the globe associated with their gods. And some not quite so well-trodden. At the end of the sixth century BCE, 29-year-old Siddhartha Gotama, better known as the Buddha, left behind his wife and newborn child in what is now Nepal, donning the yellow robes of a monk, and walked and walked for six years until he achieved enlightenment. The tree under which it happened is now the pre-eminent place of pilgrimage for the world's Buddhists.

All faiths embrace, to varying degrees, the concept of pilgrimage. Islam makes the journey to Mecca for *hajj* a religious obligation. Fuelling the physical efforts of those who make such treks has been the hope, sometimes nurtured in silence, other times loudly chanted or sung, that at journey's end there will dawn some new understanding or perspective on everyday existence and human-ity's place in a bigger scheme. Or, at the very least, a sense of being touched by divine forces that in that particular location will be much more accessible than in the daily routine of life. All such sites are regarded as thin places, set apart from the world, moving to a different drum, and possessed of an innately special atmosphere because of their connection to another, higher dimension. When there, the distinction between the visible and the invisible can fade, and a door open onto another mind-set.

Again, I say this with the benefit of hindsight. I could hardly have articulated it in such terms back then, much less associated what I was doing by going to Lourdes with this global movement. Our by-the-Good-Book religion lessons in the late 1970s stretched little further than the stark Q&A formulas of the Penny Catechism. Moreover, there were on our trip concessions to modernity that distanced it from those earlier generations of pilgrims. We weren't donning sackcloth and ashes to trudge the distance on foot over several weeks, and we weren't carrying palm leaves – in memory of Jesus' triumphant entry in Jerusalem – as our medieval forerunners would have, causing them to be referred to as palmers. Instead, in just two days, we sped in comfort down the *autoroute* in the school's minibus, grateful to have been spared wearing our uniform.

Yet, in other significant ways, the experience mirrored that of the godly folk on their way to the cathedral city of Canterbury whose tales Geoffrey Chaucer recounted at the end of the fourteenth century in what remains the most celebrated account of pilgrimage in literature. Like them, we weren't exactly pious, but still tied to the apron strings of the Church – that's what a Christian Brothers' education did for you. And we enjoyed the companionship of the road, while also sharing an expectation that what lay ahead would be somehow momentous.

And it was, and remains imprinted on my memory almost four decades later. Lourdes was unlike anywhere I had ever been before, its character defined principally by the presence of so many sick people who had come to be cured, often after doctors had given up on them. All that was needed was faith, they told us repeatedly, and their example made an impact. When we returned home a week later, I was full of reverent resolutions to change, and awash with bottles of holy water, in gaudy pale blue plastic containers, shaped like the Virgin Mary. I even brought back what passed on my modest budget for the sort of relic of saints that medieval pilgrims had treasured – a large glossy picture of the embalmed dead body of Bernadette in a glass tomb. I pinned it to my bedroom wall in the hope that it would keep me true to my new-found sense of purpose, and planned to sign up the following summer as a helper at Lourdes, assisting the sick as they were lowered into the healing waters.

I never made it back. There were too many other experiences to crowd in. There have been pilgrimages to other places since, the product of a modest residual faith laced with lashings of curiosity, but never of such intensity as that first one. I had always assumed that it was me whose perspective had altered, but half-a-dozen years ago, I suddenly realized that it was actually pilgrimages themselves – and those who went on them – that were changing. After a book event in the Lake District, I was being driven the half-an-hour to the nearest railway station by a volunteer from the local literary festival, when she mentioned that she was just back from crossing two mountain ranges while walking the length of the Camino, the thousand-year-old route to Santiago de Compostela in northwestern Spain.

She spoke about the opportunity it had afforded her for sustained, life-enhancing exercise, to explore at first hand the history and culture of the regions she was ever-so-slowly crossing on foot, to feel a genuine at-one-ness with the environment, and to escape with all she needed in a single rucksack from the sundry distractions and paraphernalia of modern life. The rhythm of putting one foot in front of the other all day had, she enthused, allowed her to make space in an otherwise overfull head for deeper reflection. Some of what she described resonated with what I recalled of Lourdes, but a lot didn't. For a start, religion had played no part in inspiring her to go on pilgrimage. It was only later, when I was thinking through what she had told me, and writing down a list of her stated motivations, that I realized that they could be neatly calibrated as the four essential Es of a new generation of pilgrims – Exercise, Exploration, Environment and Escape.

Suddenly, I started hearing similar stories everywhere I went, about the appeal of the Camino itself, which has seen a huge upturn in numbers from just five a day in the mid-1980s to almost a thousand nowadays, but also about other pilgrimage destinations all around the world. Even Lourdes, I discovered, was becoming popular with non-Catholics, unthinkable in my day. Long-lost pilgrim routes were being rediscovered and repopulated by a new breed of travellers. In some cases, they needed literally to be unearthed so unused or repurposed had they become. Their stories, in Europe and North and South America, are told in the chapters that follow, as are those of existing pathways in Asia that adjusted their focus in reaction to a new, broader spirit of pilgrimage at large. In it all, however, there remained an insistent question that linked each individual tale. Why, in our otherwise markedly secular and sceptical times, especially in the developed world where numbers of those who describe themselves as religious is in rapid decline, are people actively seeking out places whose history is soaked in the sort of faith that is anathema to them?

The standard answer I was given many times is that tourism is the new religion, and pilgrimage just a new name for tourism. For pilgrimage read adventure holiday, and for pilgrim read hiker, which is exactly what the eagle-eyed English writer Alan Bennett did when visiting the medieval abbey of Moissac in southwest France. He had spotted, he wrote in his diary, what he took to be a group on a walking holiday, but they turned out to be pilgrims on the early stages of the Camino. He couldn't detect the differ-ence. '[They] look exactly like the eager middle-aged walkers we see at home,' he complained, 'where their pilgrimage is to the top of Ingleborough' [the peak near his Yorkshire village].[1]

There is a nice irony in this conflation of tourists and pilgrims since the origins of the modern travel industry lie, in part at least, in pilgrimage. Both are about groups of individuals setting off in some sort of organized, overseen fashion, on tried and trusted trails, with a place to stay for the night included, and a guide in the party, to visit somewhere far removed from home where they hope they will feel better. But the two are not the same. Pilgrimage is a word that should be used with care, not thrown around lightly in glossy travel brochures. It signals more than a ramble through foreign countryside with friends, more than a chance to get healthy and do some sight-seeing into the bargain. Pilgrim routes and shrines, as I had found out on that youthful trip to Lourdes, and have witnessed many times since, are more than an alternative for the adventurous to the usual annual holiday destinations.

There is, whether the twenty-first-century pilgrim wants to connect with it or not, a transcendent dimension that is bound up with pilgrimage. It doesn't matter if those setting out on the route have little or no interest in religion, or more widely in faith, or to extend it further still, in that vague, immediately attractive cousin of both of the above, namely spirituality. Walking along a pilgrim road opens us to a legacy that reaches beyond firmer muscles and toned bodies. Significant numbers of those who walk the Camino, and who are among the more than 50 per cent of them who disclaim the label of religious, nonetheless talk of how the experience leaves them changed. A handful go the full distance and convert – or return – to Catholicism. For others the shift can be something much smaller, and harder to register. Of the roughly quarter of a million tourists/hikers/pilgrims who turn up from home and abroad each year at York Minister, mother church of Christianity in northern England since the seventh century, nine in ten arrive by their own admission with no conscious intention of saying a prayer. The building is a glorious museum to them. Yet nearly half subsequently report having been sufficiently moved, once inside, by something they struggle to name that they light a candle or leave a written prayer.[2]

Still more head home from the Camino with a new appetite to explore other similar routes for their next vacation, rather than revert to a conventional hiking challenge. The 1,200-year-old Buddhist trail around eighty-eight temples on the island of Shikoku in Japan is a particularly popular next step with Camino veterans. The two now have a formal link at official level.

A better explanation for the renaissance of pilgrimage is required. This, after all, was a practice that, forty years ago in Europe at least, was ebbing away like Matthew Arnold's 'Sea of Faith' but without the 'melancholy, long, withdrawing roar'.[3] One starting point is to identify the root cause of the return of pilgrimage as something in the ether of our uncertain times. Banking crashes, the rise of populism, seemingly insoluble conflicts and terrifying pandemics individually and collectively are causing us to question the very foundations on which our post-religion twenty-first-century lives are built. Our belief in what until recently was taken to be inevitable progress of science and humanity – and hence the marginalization of faith – has been stopped in its tracks. When the going gets tough, history teaches time and again, people give religion a second look.

Yet can that really be happening in a world where – in its more developed parts, at least – religion is now often publicly shunned and often disparaged? Politicians proclaim that they 'don't do God' as a way of courting votes. Well, yes, in the sense that it is usually the denominations that are most disliked, for their past misdeeds, for their inflexible rules about morality, and the reluctance of their (usually predominantly male) leaders to join wider society in treating women as equals and celebrating same-sex relationships. Religion, though, isn't just about denomination, and another recent and parallel development has been for ever greater numbers of people to feel liberated to explore faith and grace in whatever ways they choose, free from any institutional constraint or allegiance. It is seen in the significant numbers who, when questioned, say they believe in an afterlife, or in angels. And it is, arguably, there too in modern pilgrimage. It may require some element of embracing the companionship of others, but it certainly no longer demands any signing up to a particular religious tradition, much less the club's code of conduct. In that way, it is something fine-tuned to the spirit of the age.

And of any age. With its essential intertwining of arduous journey and openness to personal transformation, it fulfils an intrinsic need in the human condition. As Matsuo Basho, the most famous poet of the Edo period in seventeenth-century Japan wrote in a country that then, as now, strongly embraces pilgrimage: 'Every day is a journey and the journey itself home.'

The return of pilgrimage is, then, something simultaneously ancient and modern, a tradition whose time may just have come round again – albeit with some necessary adjustments. One is to ditch the caricature that all old-style pilgrims were unbearably pious and joyless when compared to the new generation. Though the holier-than-thou types do still tend to gather at traditional shrines, they were never the whole story. As Chaucer repeatedly points out, the ostensible religious motivations of his medieval pilgrims were inextricably wrapped up with eagerness to see new places and an appetite to immerse themselves for a short time in the carefree, sometimes even bawdy band.

Pilgrimage, past and present, has to be seen as a sub-section of a bigger and even longer human impulse that might be called 'walking with a purpose'. And walking is definitely making a comeback, which is happening for reasons that have nothing to do with religion, but which overlap it. In its most familiar political form – the protest march – walking is today being deployed with new enthusiasm against entrenched power, usually but not always in favour of openness, the individual and civil society. Right now, that can make walking a perfect statement of intent in a world so deeply in hock to planes, boats, trains and – most damagingly of all – cars that the planet itself is being destroyed. 'The walker toiling along a road toward some distant place is one of the most compelling and universal images of what it means to be human,' writes the American academic and activist Rebecca Solnit in her history of walking, 'depicting the individual as small and solitary in a large world, reliant on the strength of body and will'.[4]

The walker is using the very legs that our globalized world appears to regard as obsolete – in their original purpose as a way of getting around – in order to register above all their protest at the environmental degradation that is causing climate change. It is not an especially giant stride, then, to harness that same ecological imperative to pilgrimage, where you get to immerse yourself in landscapes that an earlier generation of pilgrims believed so extraordinary that they must have been created by a divine hand.

It is a connection that the European Green Pilgrimage Network now exists to nurture, but the relationship between stewardship of creation and religious experience is as old as the hills over which the pilgrim routes pass. 'As I walked,' wrote the Jesuit Gerard Hughes about his on-foot pilgrimage to Jerusalem, 'I began to recover a sense of wonder at nature and a feeling of one-ness with it. The bleak, bare frozen countryside became comforting, especially if I were feeling tired and low in spirit, because I knew that under the bleak surface new life was preparing to break through in spring.'[5]

Exhausting your body by walking long distances should, logically, dull the mind, too. What the history of pilgrimage shows, however, is the opposite, an intuitive truth. By pushing your limbs to the limit, theologians and mystics alike taught, the dominance of our bodies could be tamed, leaving the pilgrim free to concentrate on the otherwise elusive soul. So keen, indeed, were early Christian pilgrims to shake off bodily constraints on their spiritual potential that they grew addicted to putting themselves in the way of danger, walking to shrines on islands that can only be reached by navigating tricky or unpredictable currents. Being plain exhausted, being at risk of drowning, or just stilling and silencing the brain as you tramped along was judged perfect for turning your thoughts upwards to the god or gods in the heavens.

Today that has been amended. The effort of twenty-first-century pilgrimage directs thoughts inwards, as mountains are climbed, kilometres clocked up and blisters endured. Everything is done at walking pace, in contrast to a world that, now more than ever, is ceaselessly rushing ahead faster than we can quite compute. So on pilgrimage progress can also be measured in self-exploration and self-knowledge achieved. That then opens the possibility, for some at least, as they tramp along ancient routes connected with faith, to access that unformed presence which might even in an age of disbelief have been hovering at the edge of their senses. To catch a glimpse of the transcendent, otherwise impossible in the hustle-bustle and hassle of modern life, requires making one almighty and counter-intuitive effort – like going on pilgrimage in a secular age.

There are, of course, many other ways in the absence or exile of organized religion to reach out for some half-suspected 'other' dimension: endurance runners, extreme cyclists or mountain climbers often talk of how their activities take them to another, higher plain. So, too, can those returning from the Glastonbury music festival or an evening in a concert hall, or an angel workshop.

There are many roads, but pilgrimage is less extreme, more mainstream, than many – though it is still quirky enough to raise an eyebrow. 'You? Going on pilgrimage? I'd never have suspected.' With its long history, and extraordinary spiritual geography, it continues to lend itself to the search for meaning.

CHAPTER 1

SANTIAGO DE COMPOSTELA
THE CAMINO

❋

'The Camino isn't a speed competition or a race
Rather it's a pathway of brotherhood and universality.'

PILGRIM INSCRIPTION IN TRIACASTELA CHURCH ON THE CAMINO[1]

'I'm taking a really long walk.' That is how Martin Sheen's character, bluff eye-doctor Tom Avery, explains away his out-of-the-blue
decision to follow the ancient Camino from the French Pyrenees
to Santiago de Compostela in Galicia in northwestern Spain in the
popular 2010 film, *The Way*. His real reason, though, lies in the
trauma of the death of his only son while himself undertaking
the Camino. And then there are Tom's three fellow travellers, all
of whom he meets on the pilgrim route. This unlikely trio is trying
to get away from troubles in their own lives, but simultaneously
hoping that the experience will help them find new ways of coping
when they return: one a writer who can no longer write; another a
Dutchman keen to lose weight to rescue his relationship; and the
third a fragile free spirit nowhere near as resourceful as she appears.

It takes each of them the length of the 800-kilometre section of the trail they walk to come to understand the others, and themselves, in part through the away-from-the-real-world atmosphere on the Camino and constant exposure to others on parallel searches, but also through the lightly worn spiritual resonances that are part and parcel of this pilgrimage.

The commercial success of the film owed much to its release coinciding with annual numbers of *peregrinos* on the Camino that year reaching a record modern-day high of 300,000. At the time, it felt like a milestone. Such had been the rapid revival of interest in this medieval pilgrim route that it was being talked about as one of the great European cultural events of the last years of the twentieth century and the first of the twenty-first.

The early decades of the twentieth century had witnessed a steep decline in Santiago's fortunes, mirroring those of the pre-dominantly farming-and-fishing Galicia region in general that saw over a million people leave for a better life in the Americas. After his victory in Spain's civil war of the 1930s, the dictator General Francisco Franco – himself a native of Galicia – tried to breathe new life into the Route of Saint James, as the Camino is often known in more overtly religious circles. One motive was boosting the local economy, but part too linked in with a wider project of his to harness Spanish nationalism and a conservative variety of Catholicism to the task of sustaining his own fascist ideology and hence his stranglehold on power. With Franco's death in 1975, and the return to democracy and pluralism in Spain, that driver, however, evaporated, and Santiago was once more in the doldrums.

By 1986, the year that post-Franco Spain signalled a new political dawn by joining the European Union, the Pilgrims' Bureau in Santiago – the place that issues the certificates, still written in Latin and known as *compostelas*, to everyone who has completed more than 100 kilometres of the route – handed out just 1,800 over the entire course of a year. New EU investment, however, was targeted at modernizing tourism infrastructure all the way along the route – secured as much by French efforts to bolster their end of the trail that they know as the *Camino Frances* or 'French Way' as by Spanish enthusiasm. As a result, by the late 1980s, numbers on the Camino had been showing a marked rise, with the new generation of *peregrinos* an intriguing mix. That is what *The Way* captured so well. Some may have had some sort of claim to the traditional prerequisite of being Catholic (the actor, Martin Sheen, is himself a devout Catholic), albeit that many now regarded the Church of their upbringing as benignly irrelevant, or worse. Many more had no formal connection at all to any form of organized religion. So what was attracting them?

Part of the renaissance was that walkers – and the growing number who covered most of the route by bike – were drawn by the 1,000-year history of the Camino. This was also a time when television audiences were flocking to documentaries by a new breed of walking/talking history dons with a knack for bringing the past to life. The walk across northern Spain, then, became an activity holiday that included the chance to experience medieval history first-hand. But the revival was also fed by deeper anxieties. 'When pilgrims begin to walk,' suggests the writer Nancy Louise Frey of her observations on the Camino, 'several things start to happen to their perceptions of the world, which continue over the course of the journey: they develop a changing sense of time, a heightening of the senses, and a new awareness of their bodies and the landscape ... A young German man expressed it this way: "In the experience of walking, each step is a thought. You can't escape yourself."'[2]

Once they start thinking in such terms while on a track with a long history of being a place 'where prayer has been valid', as T. S. Eliot memorably put it in 'Little Gidding' (inspired by his 1936 pilgrimage to what had once been a high-minded seventeenth-century religious community), the walkers couldn't so easily disentangle the spiritual from the history and health elements, the pleasure of companionship with strangers in a shared endeavour, and the spectacular landscape.

There followed many published accounts of this 'new era' on the Camino that chronicle how its original religious purpose somehow resonated with the new generation of walkers, and how they then shaped that experience into 57 varieties of bespoke spirituality. In 1987, *O Diário de um Mago* (entitled *The Pilgrimage* in English), a novel by the global bestselling Brazilian esoteric writer Paulo Coelho, set the ball rolling. Based on his time on the Camino, he successfully gave the whole undertaking a makeover for his New Age-inclined audience.

This broadening impetus further accelerated in 1993 – the date chosen as the 1,000th anniversary of the rediscovery of the tomb of Saint James (Sant-Iago) – when the route was declared a UNESCO World Heritage Site. As a result, its hostels and footpaths were given a major overhaul, with distinctive yellow signage branded with the ancient pilgrims' symbol, the scallop shell. Annual numbers of walkers continued to climb, as did the quantity of popular accounts that contributed to widening its appeal. In her 2000 memoir, *The Camino: A Journey of the Spirit*, the Oscar-winning American actress and New Age guru Shirley MacLaine framed her time in Spain not as a religious pilgrimage but 'a mythological and imaginative experience'. It was, she wrote, essentially a 'walking meditation', along what she said were the ley lines that the route followed, which communicated the spiritual energy of the earth. She characterized what she had gained from it as an opportunity to 'walk backwards in time to a place that began the experiences that made me and the human race what we have become today', and concluded that as a result her journey turned out to be 'the end of a big part of my life and the beginning of a new one'.

That is quite a recommendation. Equally high-profile was the similarly before-and-after tale told in 2006 by the well-known German comedian and actor Hape Kerkeling. Raised as a Catholic, he had turned his back on institutional religion and become a fierce critic of it. In *I'm Off Then: Losing and Finding Myself on the Camino de Santiago,* which has sold three million copies in his home country and has been translated into many other languages, he sets off sending up the traditional pilgrims he encounters on the route. But as the soles on his walking shoes wear down, his narrative becomes an account of his reconnection with a personal God, if not with official Catholicism.

Since *The Way* came out in 2010, the Camino has only become more popular. Numbers grew to 327,378 in 2018.[3] Questioned by the Pilgrims' Bureau as they received their prized *compostelas,* just 43 per cent of *peregrinos* today use the word 'religious' to describe their motivation. Nine per cent opt instead for 'cultural'. The remainder go for a mishmash of phrases, altogether vaguer and catch-all, typically referencing aspects of religion and culture, as well as history and even health.[4] And if this testifies to one aspect of its diversity, another is revealed by the demographics of those managing at least 100 kilometres of the Camino: 55 per cent in the 30–60 range, 27 per cent under 30 (an age-group disproportionately likely in our secular, sceptical times to steer clear of anything religious), and 18 per cent over 60.[5] The genius of the revived Camino, it seems, is it is big enough, long enough and flexible enough in its own identity to accommodate all comers.

❊

Perhaps it was always thus. The Camino in the Middle Ages has been described as 'the busiest trunk road in Christendom'.[6] It is estimated that, back then, half a million people would walk the Camino each year, decked out in the typical pilgrims' uniform of the time, a long tunic (sclavein) and a wide-brimmed hat turned up at the front and attached at the back to a long scarf that was then wound around the body to keep it in place, with a scrip (or leather pouch) hanging from their waist to carry their money and other essential possessions. They also had a wooden staff with metal tip, to assist on uneven paths, and to see off any predatory animals looking for supper (wolves were top of the list of must-be-avoided-at-all-cost). Not all of these *peregrinos*, though, were true believers. Then, as now, they were drawn from far beyond the boundaries of Iberia. Among them was Chaucer's Wife of Bath, a cloth-maker and businesswoman who, the Prologue to the *Canterbury Tales* tells us, had also been on pilgrimages to Jerusalem, Rome, Cologne (to see what was reputed to be the tomb of the Three Kings who visit the Infant Jesus) as well as Santiago.

She hadde passed many a straunge strem;
[...] she hadde been [...]
In Galice at Seint-Jame...
She koude muchel of wandrynge by the weye.
Gat-tothed was she, soothly for to seye.

Chaucer mocks her worldliness by making it clear she wandered so far from home not because she was especially pious, but because she was looking for a good time. And other accounts of those who undertook the Camino in these centuries reveal a range of motivations.

There were priests, monks and even well-to-do parishioners sent there on the orders of their bishop or superior as punishment – for their ungodly behaviour, or their doubts that there was even a God. The goal was to achieve redemption by the hard slog of walking, and by standing at journey's end in the presence of the relics of one of Jesus' apostles. And then there were others who headed off to Galicia on their own initiative, precisely to avoid having their lives shaped or dictated by overbearing, interfering clergy in the stifling daily world of their local parish, where all religious knowledge and authority resided in those who were ordained. As Jonathan Sumption writes in his history of medieval pilgrimage, 'a surprisingly large number of pilgrims seem to have left their homes solely in order to deny their parish priest his monopoly over their spiritual welfare. Contemporary churchmen frequently accused them of seeking to confess to a strange priest to avoid the moral censure which they deserved.'[7] The first pilgrims started arriving in Santiago as early as the seventh century, according to some accounts, but veneration of Saint James in the city that is named after him really seems to have got going in or around 812. That was the year when the pious Alfonso II of the Asturias (the kingdom that then covered a large portion of northern Spain) paid a visit to view the recently rediscovered tomb of the apostle. Known popularly as Alfonso the Chaste, he gave his royal blessing to the cult that was growing up around it. Soon or shortly thereafter, the city started to be known as Santiago de Compostela.

There are various theories as to the Latin origins of the word *compostela*. One contends that it derives from *campus stellae* or 'field of the star', referring to a local legend that the remains of Saint James were first uncovered by a hermit in the soil of Galicia after he had been directed to a particular spot by a star from heaven. Another is more practical – *composita tella* means the burial ground or site of the saint. And in similar vein, it might come from *compositella* or 'well-composed one', an allusion to the alleged miraculously well-preserved state of the corpse of the saint. There is, however, no consensus as to which of the three is most likely, a lack of clarity that extends to so much of the story told about the shrine itself, and of the Camino, and which is part of its appeal.

The favoured narrative of the Church authorities has long been that Saint James was originally buried somewhere else in northwest Spain in the first century AD, and that his remains were subsequently unearthed in the ninth century, when they were placed in an ornate tomb in what was then Santiago's cathedral (subsequently replaced by the building visitors see today). Pilgrims then started arriving from far and wide – relics being highly prized in medieval Christianity as a source for miracle cures and storing up merit in heaven. It was only at the very end of the eleventh century, however, that Santiago gained its first bishop, a measure of official ecclesiastical approval of the development of a substantial pilgrim site. The second incumbent, Diego Gelmírez, was such an enthusiastic and vigorous promoter of the cult of Saint James (and of the pilgrim trade that accompanied it) that he was quickly promoted to the rank of Archbishop.

Monsignor Gelmírez also provided another building block in the Santiago story, its foundation text, in the form of the early twelfth-century *Historia Compostelana*, believed to be written by one of his assistants. It blends the local legend with the accounts found in three of the four gospels of the New Testament about James the Greater, a fisherman, one of two brothers in Jesus' inner circle (there was another James in the twelve, referred to as James the Less). He is the first of the apostles to be martyred for his faith – beheaded by the Jewish puppet king, Herod, to please his subjects. In a distinctly Spanish Catholic tradition, however, as set out in *Historia Compostelana*, before his final confrontation with Herod James had travelled to the furthest western point of Europe to bring the Good News to its people, and to make converts, as part of the missionary push led by Paul and Peter that followed straight after Jesus' death. It was only when James then returned from Galicia to Jerusalem that he died.

As a narrative, it roughly equates to the tale that, again in the medieval period, drew pilgrims to Glastonbury in England. Similarly unsubstantiated, it tells of how another of Jesus' disciples, Joseph of Arimathea (who in the gospels gave his tomb to be used for Jesus' body when taken down from the Cross) had around 60 CE sailed to what was then an island in the middle of marshes in the southwest of England, and planted a thorn from the crown of thorns that had been placed on Jesus' head at the crucifixion.[8] That thorn blossomed into the first of a still-continuing series of 'holy' thorn trees, which inspired the building of the earliest of several abbeys at Glastonbury in the fifth century, with a chapel dedicated to Saint Joseph of Arimathea, and then drew pilgrims from Wales and Ireland as well as the rest of England along pathways that are still identifiable.

It was a living Saint Joseph who is said to have visited Glastonbury, but it is the tomb of Saint James that lies at the heart of the Spanish legend, with the apostle's body brought back by boat to the coast of Galicia after his death. One version has this repatriation of his remains being made in the care of two angels, in a rudderless ship that miraculously survives being wrecked many times before reaching the shore of northwest Spain. And it is the same ghostly ship that also appears in two of the three explanations given for why the scallop shell became the symbol of the Camino. In one, the ship is passing the Spanish coast as a knight falls off a cliff. Instead of drowning, his life is miraculously saved by proximity to the saint's remains, and he emerges from the sea covered head to foot in scallop shells – which are found in abundance along this part of the Galician shoreline. In a second version, a wedding is taking place on a beach as the ship appears on the horizon. The groom (in some accounts the bride) arrives on horseback, but the presence of the vessel piloted by angels spooks the beast and it heads into the sea with its rider strapped to the saddle. S/he, too, is saved by the sea-borne presence of Saint James's body and returns to the wedding ceremony bedecked in scallop shells.

The most familiar derivation of the scallop symbol, though, appears in the tale of how the ship bringing Saint James's remains from Jerusalem was wrecked out at sea. Its precious cargo miraculously survived and was washed up undamaged on the shore, encrusted in a protective layer of scallop shells. Quite when and how they then emerged as the symbol of the Camino is again foggy. Some medieval pilgrims are said to have travelled on from Santiago to the sea at Cape Finisterre, the most westerly point on this coast (along what was originally a pagan trail to what was then, as the name suggests, the end of the known world). They did so in remembrance of the journey the saint's body had taken, in the opposite direction, from ship to Santiago's cathedral. And to prove they had gone the extra mile, they would bring back a scallop shell from Finisterre with them.

The shell was, in this incarnation, both reward and souvenir. Pilgrims took their shells home with them as a symbol of the grace they had obtained by making the pilgrimage. Some are even said to have treasured them unto death and had them buried with them, as something to present at the gates of heaven to prove the strength of their belief in life. The shell has also subsequently evolved into a symbol of pilgrimage in general, as invoked in 'The Passionate Man's Pilgrimage', a poem by Sir Walter Ralegh, a favourite at the court of Queen Elizabeth I. He is supposed to have written it in 1603 as he neared death, likening the journey taken by pilgrims in search of God to the journey of life towards eternal reward.

> *Give me my scallop shell of quiet,*
> *My staff of faith to walk upon,*
> *My scrip of joy, immortal diet,*
> *My bottle of salvation,*
> *My gown of glory, hope's true gage,*
> *And thus I'll take my pilgrimage.*

✵

One particular aspect of the Camino that appeals to modern-day pilgrims is its effortless transcending of national boundaries. Two in three of those who take the Camino Frances route to Santiago choose to start their trek at the well-connected Spanish town of Sarria in Galicia, just 100 kilometres, about eight days' walk, from their final destination. Yet that leaves one in three to set out on their journey not on Spanish soil, but from the French side of the Pyrenees, embracing the history of the Camino as both French and Spanish. Today what is routinely described as the 'Full Camino' begins around thirty-five days' walk from the tomb of Saint James at the small French town of Saint-Jean-Pied-de-Port (Saint-John-at-the-Foot-of-the-Pass) in the shadow of the Pyrenees. It is just 8 kilometres from the Spanish border, which is crossed on the Roncevaux Pass as it climbs up 1,000 metres through the mountains, and then comes down into Spain at the Augustinian monastery of Roncesvalles. Here hospitality has been offered to pilgrims for ten centuries.

For the medieval pilgrim there were no cars, trains and planes to facilitate short cuts on the Camino – as today via Sarria, or another popular alternative, the Portuguese Camino from Porto, which covers the 260 kilometres to Santiago in about two weeks (fitting more neatly into the restrictions of taking annual leave). So, for the likes of the Wife of Bath, the four possible starting points were all in France: the capital, Paris, at the Church of Saint Jacques (Saint James) in the Rue de Rivoli, of which only its tower remains following anti-clerical attacks in the French Revolution; Vézelay, in the wine country of Burgundy, with its shrine to Mary Magdalene; Le Puy, further south still; and Arles, in the Languedoc region of southern France, the favoured route for those travelling from Italy. The first three all converge at Saint-Jean-Pied-de-Port and make the total distance to be covered nearer 1,200 kilometres.

The initial enthusiasm that fuelled the development of Santiago, and drew in others from further afield, was distinctly Spanish – though of course no such entity as Spain existed at that time. Instead, the rise of the cult of Saint James was rooted in Galicia's status as a stronghold of Christianity in the Iberian Peninsula after its conquest by Islamic forces, which had arrived from North Africa in 711. The *Reconquista* – the drive to expel its Moorish rulers from Christian Spain – took until 1492, but the fight back began from the north, where the Moors only briefly held sway. While King Alfonso II, who ordered the building of the first cathedral in Santiago, was undoubtedly genuine in his religious enthusiasm for the relics of Saint James, he was also sufficiently political to see the benefits of encouraging the growing cult of Saint James in the city as a means of creating a Christian rival to Córdoba in the south, the centre of the Umayyad caliphate, which boasted among its religious treasures what was purported to be an arm of the Prophet Muhammad. In the same calculation would surely have figured the notion of the Camino as both a physical manifestation of the shared faith of the various Christian rulers of northern

Spain *and* a symbol in the fight to reclaim the whole country for the Church. So successful did this symbolism prove that the word 'Santiago' became a rallying cry for the Christian forces when they confronted the Moors on the battlefields. Some of the images of Saint James still to be seen in churches and shrines along the Camino to this day depict him not only just as a benign spreader of the good news of the gospel, but also as '*Santiago Matamoros*' ('Saint James the Moor-slayer'), with his Muslim victims trampled under the hoofs of his steed.

Yet the Camino's rise to prominence in medieval Europe was not just about the fight for territory going on in Spain. It also owed something to political changes happening elsewhere. The already established pilgrimage routes across Europe from England, the Low Countries and northern Germany to the original Christian centres of Rome and Jerusalem had grown increasingly treacherous to walk in the instability that gripped Europe after the death in 814 of Charlemagne, who had united most of western and central Europe. Military and political conflicts swept back and forth across the continent, bringing war, plunder and devastation, and leaving marauding armies and bands of mercenary soldiers on the loose. Pilgrims too often were seen by such men as a soft target to be robbed and worse. The Camino, by contrast, offered greater security, its French section well away from the general European theatre of war, and its Spanish leg, largely following an existing Roman trading route through northern Spain, securely within the Christian-ruled section of the peninsula.

The upswing in medieval pilgrims seeking a safer alternative to Rome or Jerusalem encouraged the French in particular to facilitate the founding by monastic orders or guilds of the abbeys, churches and hostels that continue to line the Way. Not all *peregrinos*, then as now, welcomed the distraction of others. There have always been those on the Camino who prefer to search for God in solitude, just as the first Christian monks had done in their thousands in the third century when they headed out into the Sinai Desert to live as hermits and ascetics, eschewing all worldly comforts. The devout and penitential on Camino in medieval times went solo, barefoot, and sought shelter in *refugios* of the most rudimentary kind.

Most of their contemporaries, however, like modern tourists, preferred to travel in groups, not just for mutual protection, but also for company. They walked together, and crowded into the same accommodation together, the better off bagging the beds, while those with empty scrips made do with straw. That communal experience was – and remains as *The Way* well illustrates – a central part of pilgrimage on the Camino. In a world where we have come ever more to see ourselves as individuals, where contact with others is via electronic means, walking the Camino offers the antidote. It is all about rubbing shoulders with strangers on the route, as the medieval pilgrims would have, sharing prayers, dormitories and blister cures, seeing themselves as part of something bigger than their individual homelands. As the German poet and playwright, Johann Wolfgang von Goethe is said to have remarked, 'Europe was born on the pilgrim road to Santiago.'

You might also argue that the medieval pilgrimage was in some ways the precursor of the modern package tour. Or, to extend the thought further, that today's tourism is, in some respects, a substitute for religion. The lines of contemporary sightseers processing round art galleries, museums and historic monuments are, in this perspective, replacing the processions of pilgrims. The cultural capital that visitors believe is accumulated by their visits to museums is roughly analogous to the spiritual grace that used to be stored up by medieval pilgrims journeying to churches and shrines. And both past and present travellers carry with them essential reading – current guidebooks take the place of the prayer books that *peregrinos* would have carried with them.

Let's not get carried away, though. If the parallels are there, then equally how different the Camino must have been in the eleventh and twelfth centuries from anything to be experienced by today's tourists, even today's *peregrinos*. There would, for example, have been no metalled roads, no traffic, and hence very little noise. Yes, there are still, by modern design, places on the route where the marked footpaths are far enough away from twenty-first-century detritus to reward walkers with silence in which to drink in the often sublimely beautiful landscape they are traversing. Yet there are also sections where the view is of industrial complexes, as at Ponferrada in the province of León, or where modern highways have to be crossed, or where – especially in the later stages – pilgrims are buffeted by the proximity of speeding cars and thundering lorries.

The other appeal of the Camino to present-day pilgrims, whether spiritual seekers, experience junkies, or history buffs, is the opportunities it offers as it intersects with other attractions. When it passes through Pamplona, the first big city on the Camino in Spain, the route crosses the street where they run the bulls in the annual week-long fiesta of San Fermín in July, immortalized by Ernest Hemingway in his 1926 novel, *The Sun Also Rises*. Or, at the other end of the spectrum of crowd-pullers, there is the village of O Cebreiro, where the resident population of a few dozen is regularly outnumbered by the pilgrims passing through or staying in the 100-bed *alberque* there. High in the Sierra de Ancares, between the provinces of León and Lugo, O Cebreiro is at the top of the last big climb before walkers reach the rolling hills of Galicia. It is of both archaeological interest – it contains surviving examples of *pallozas*, circular stone cottages whose design is said to predate Roman times – and religious significance, as the home to a miraculous shrine that is a spin-off from the Camino. In the early years of the fourteenth century, a doubting monk was saying mass there when the bread and wine used at the eucharist to represent the body and blood of Christ is said to have actually turned to flesh and blood. The miraculous host is preserved in a special container, given in the late fifteenth century by Queen Isabella of Castile, unifier of Spain. Three times a year, pilgrims can join the handful of locals as it is taken in procession through the streets.

Then there are what might be called branch lines of the Camino – though those who use such language in Oviedo to describe the Camino de San Salvador will be swiftly rebuked. This city was Alfonso II's capital, and where he stored his collection of religious relics in the Holy Chamber of its Cathedral of the Holy Saviour (San Salvador). That cache was enough to make it a place of pilgrimage in its own right in the Middle Ages. 'He who goes to Santiago and not to Oviedo visits the servant and not the Lord', some locals still can be heard to say. The Camino de San Salvador – 120 kilometres in length and by repute rather more 'off-the-beaten-track' than the other routes to Santiago – starts in the cathedral city of León, crosses the Cordillera Mountains, and finishes in Oviedo, where after visiting the cathedral and its relics, pilgrims can join another of the mainstream routes, the Camino Primitivo, on their way west.

The Camino has become the ultimate heritage trail. Some of it is both historical and self-referential, as at the Cruz de Ferro, a landmark iron cross on the route between the towns of Foncebadón and Manjarín, just over 200 kilometres from Santiago. On top of a tall wooden pole, the latest incarnation of a long line of wooden poles on this spot said to date back to the eleventh century (though some say its origins go further back to a pre-Christian Celtic monument), there is a large iron cross. It is a replica of an original now preserved in the Camino Museum in Astorga. The tradition is that pilgrims either bring stones with them from their home country, or pick one up on the Camino, and then discard them here, as a symbol of letting go of their past troubles and opening themselves to change.

For walkers, as well as the natural beauty of the open country-side, there is also a sprinkling of architectural wonders, including Burgos, with its lavishly endowed abbey of Las Huelgas, or León itself where, next to its Gothic cathedral, what was once a magnificent pilgrim hostel now houses a five-star hotel. Some attractions unrelated to the Camino are nevertheless on its route. For those who take El Camino del Norte – the Northern Way, which departs from the main Camino Frances route to opt for the coast of the Basque Country and Cantabria – there is in the town of Comillas an unexpected outpost of early twentieth-century Catalan Modernism with a fantasy villa, El Capricho, designed by the devoutly Catholic architect of Barcelona's Sagrada Família church, Antoni Gaudí.

✻

Every pilgrimage has its destination, just as every mountain climb has its summit, and if the Camino's final point doesn't quite have the historical resonance of a Rome, Jerusalem or Mecca, then Santiago de Compostela can still stop walkers in their tracks when approached on foot for the first time from the east, its old city rising up above the bland modern architecture of its suburbs. The twin towers of the cathedral in particular can be seen from 5 kilometres away (on a clear day) at Monte do Gozo. Their original bells, seized in 997 when the army of the Muslim Caliph of Córdoba took Santiago, destroyed Alfonso's original building, but left the shrine of Saint James miraculously untouched (perhaps because of the presence in his ranks of many Christian vassal lords), ring out to encourage pilgrims at this penultimate staging post to summon up one last effort to reach journey's end. It took 200 years for the bells to be recaptured by Christian forces from the Aljama Mosque in Córdoba, where they were being used as oil lamps, and returned to Santiago, and to the eleventh-century cathedral that had by then risen from the ashes.

Once in the heart of Santiago's crooked city-centre streets, all roads lead to the cathedral, one of the largest Romanesque buildings in the whole of Europe. It has four façades, but most paths open into the huge, harmonious Praza del Obradoiro, dominated by the cathedral's western façade. The British novelist Rachel Billington writes in her journal of her own Camino in 1989 about the enduring impact of that first glimpse of the pilgrims' destination. 'The sun, reddish now, is angled exactly to come through the corner of the square and make the crumbling baroque façade softly glow. Green is sprouting from its orifices and its protuberances are like facial hair on an elderly person. The space is very open, no tables, just the great cathedral façade, the Bishop's Palace and Hostel of Los Reyes Catolicos.'[9] The scars of time on the western façade have been removed since, as part of a general upgrading of Santiago, but some old-timers have complained that the growing popularity of the Camino in recent years has led to a 'carnivalization' of the city. Pilgrims are encouraged to time their arrival for the high days and holy days associated with Saint James. Again, it was ever thus on such routes, Christianity hardwired by the seasons of Advent and Lent to make a virtue of the long, penitential build-up to the great feasts of Christmas and Easter.

The Camino has its own high and low seasons – April to October is the favoured time to undertake it, but that is dictated by the weather, not the religious calendar (and there is now a 'Winter's Way', taking a detour to avoid the climb to O Cereiro, that is offered by the tour companies for the fearless, or those convinced they have God on their side).

The fiesta of Saint James falls at the end of July. On the eve of his feast day, thousands gather around the cathedral for a ritual where they place their fingers in the imprints made by centuries of earlier visitors in the central column of the elaborately carved main doorway in the western façade, the Pórtico de la Gloria, dating from 1188 and where traces of the colours added over the years by over-eager custodians to the garments of the saints portrayed there can still be glimpsed. Then they proceed into the mighty interior, and up a staircase behind the high altar from where they can all but embrace the statue of the saint that dominates the cathedral, swathed in silver and gold plate, and encrusted with jewels. There is something almost pagan about the scene. On Good Friday Christians line up in their churches to kiss the feet of the representation of Jesus on the cross, but here the Son of God is sidelined and all the attention is reserved for one of his followers.

The cathedral is, like the mother-church of Catholicism, Saint Peter's in Rome, built over what is reputed to be the tomb of an apostle. So it is down into the crypt that pilgrims next go, to pay their respects and stand in front of the tomb of Saint James, the only surviving feature of the original church. And then there is the pure theatre – circus almost – that is a special feature of the liturgy in Santiago Cathedral. The world's largest censer, or incense burner, known as the *botafumeiro,* is swung backwards and forwards across the altar by six men operating an elaborate tackle of ropes and pulleys.

It is reported that, in 1499 when on her way to England, Catherine of Aragon attended mass in Santiago's cathedral. The *botafumeiro* became detached mid-swing and smashed into a window. With hindsight, it might have been taken for a sign to turn back and return home. Her first marriage to an English prince ended with his death, her second to her late husband's younger brother, Henry VIII, resulted in a divorce that caused a reformation.

For some among today's *peregrinos*, though, the experience of being there, at journey's end, in the footsteps of many millions of pilgrims over the centuries, has been known to convert them to Catholicism, or bring the lapsed back to the faith. For others there is a different sort of healing, something that prepares these pilgrims, after taking time out to walk the Camino, to re-enter and re-engage with the everyday world, strengthened by their memories, experiences and the scallop shell they carry with them.

CHAPTER 2

JERUSALEM
THE PROMISED LAND

❋

'How I rejoiced when they said to me,
"Let us go to the house of Yahweh!"
And now our feet are standing
In your gateways, Jerusalem'

<small>PSALM 122, A 'SONG OF ASCENT'
OF JEWISH PILGRIMS TO JERUSALEM</small>

When the English mystic Margery Kempe neared the end of her long pilgrimage journey to Jerusalem in the fifteenth century, she broke down in tears. To be fair, as is recounted unflinchingly in *The Book of Margery Kempe*, her account of her travels around medieval Europe, including along the Camino, she was prone to loud weeping and cries, prompted she believed by her closeness to Christ. But the sight of Jerusalem, the city of his death and resurrection, brought it on afresh, so much so, recounts the book – said to be among the earliest known autobiographies in English – that, 'she was on the point of falling off her ass'. Two German fellow pilgrims had to step in to stop her toppling. 'Sirs, I beg you,' she said, 'don't be annoyed though I weep bitterly at this holy place where our Lord Jesus Christ lived and died.'[1]

For Kempe, the wife of a well-to-do merchant from Kings Lynn in Norfolk, and the mother of fourteen children, who waited until she was 40 to explore by going on pilgrimage the mystical visions of Jesus that she had been experiencing, to arrive in Jerusalem in 1413 was nothing less than her chance to walk in the footsteps of her saviour and feel his pain. And she did it quite literally, collapsing to the ground on what had been Mount Calvary where he died on the cross, and spreading out her arms as if being crucified herself. Her heart, she wrote, was 'bursting apart'.[2] Today's pilgrims to Jerusalem are, on the whole, less flamboyant, but the aim of many remains largely the same as Kempe's, to breathe life into the gospel accounts, to lift them off the pages of the Bible, to transport them away from a story that they had imbibed in childhood at Sunday school, and to make them real.

On the whole, pilgrimage routes and destinations are typically associated with one particular faith tradition. Jerusalem is simultaneously sacred to three. Abraham, Jesus and Muhammad are all said to feature in its story. As such, it is, arguably, for more pilgrims than any other spot on earth, *the* Holy City, the natural focus for spiritual seekers.

Inside Jerusalem's walled old city, covering just one square kilometre and standing on the site where King David established a capital for the Israelites in the tenth century BCE, Jews, Christians and Muslims each have their own named quarter, even if such topographical delineations no longer accurately reflect who actually lives in each. The final one of the four is designated for the Armenians, Christians who broke with Catholic Rome in the fourth century CE. Around the same time, a group of Armenian monks settled in the southwestern corner of the Old City, between the Zion and Jaffa gates, and an Armenian community grew in the shadow of the Cathedral of Saint James, site of the martyrdom of the apostle (before his body was reputedly taken to Galicia) and seat of the Armenian patriarch. Today the numbers of Armenians there have dwindled to a few hundred.

Those first Armenian monks were part of the initial great influx of Christian pilgrims into Jerusalem. In the centuries straight after Jesus' death, the city had not been a particular focus of devotions or activity – curiously in hindsight, though the fledgling church's immediate concerns were around missionary activity and sheer survival. By the second century it had become a centre for early Christian libraries, but it was only once Christianity had found its feet as the official religion of the Roman Empire by decree of Constantine the Great in 323 CE – and the threat of persecution hanging over it had been removed – that many began to feel a strong pull to journey back to the birthplace of their faith.

For some in the West, Christianity may be synonymous with European civilization, but it is in origin a Near Eastern reform movement from within Judaism. And so these first Christian pilgrims were heading to the source of their faith, for both spiritual sustenance and bricks-and-mortar proof of the claims they heard about Jesus when they listened in their newly built churches in Europe to the gospel accounts of his life being read aloud. They wanted to walk around the sites mentioned in the narratives of Matthew, Mark, Luke and John where Jesus and his followers had been. Popular among the 'holy places' were the Via Dolorosa, along which he carried his cross to the site of his crucifixion, and the Garden of Gethsemane, where he was betrayed by one of his own to the authorities. Offering a living and visible commentary on the gospels were the Cenacle, or Upper Room, where he celebrated the Last Supper and instituted the eucharist with bread and wine, and the pool at Bethesda where, in John's gospel, he cured a man who hadn't been able to walk for thirty-eight years. Among those first waves of visitors, theirs was above all a very physical, visceral experience of pilgrimage.

Prominent among them was Constantine's deeply devout mother, Empress Helena – according to some accounts a former barmaid, later declared a Christian saint. She travelled to Jerusalem around 326 CE and did more than any other individual to establish the road-map that Christian pilgrims still follow inside and outside the city. Helena also came to build. In Rome, her son had funded the city's first churches and basilicas, including the original Saint Peter's, on top of the site of what was reputedly his grave. On her journey to Jerusalem, Constantine charged his mother with doing the same, giving her as a parting gift the equivalent of a blank cheque from the Imperial treasury to transform the city of Jesus' death and resurrection.

Once she had located the scenes of his crucifixion and his rising from the dead, Helena wasted no time in getting to work. She ordered the Roman temple that had subsequently been erected on Calvary be torn down. She replaced it with the first incarnation of the Church of the Holy Sepulchre (the current vast, crowded, labyrinthine structure dates back to 1149). If Saint Peter's in Rome was to be the seat of Church authority, Helena was determined with her building plans to make Jerusalem tangibly the true centre of the Christian world, where the Saviour had died for humankind's sins and proved his divinity by rising from the dead three days later, leaving behind an empty tomb.

In the course of the construction of that first Church of the Holy Sepulchre, Christian legend has it that fragments were unearthed of the three crosses on which Jesus had perished with two thieves, Dismas and Gestas, on either side of him. Some accounts even speak of the haul including the nails used to attach all three to the wooden structures. On such a sacred site, the temptation is to put ordinary credulity to one side, and accept rather than question, but the Empress, to her credit, is said to have required proof for the claimed connection. Through a local bishop, Macarius, a woman so sick that she was near to death was brought before Helena. Pieces from the first two unearthed crosses were placed next to the woman but had no obvious beneficial effect on her condition. When they were replaced by those from the third cross – reputedly Jesus' – the woman suddenly and inexplicably regained her health. This miraculous cure – like those that sustain so many other pilgrimage sites – caused Helena to proclaim that the 'True Cross' had indeed been found. She redoubled her efforts to rebuild Jerusalem as a city that was to be forever a monument to Christianity.

❀

Jesus, of course, was a Jew, and the Jerusalem that Empress Helena visited first and foremost told in stone the story of the Jews. Even if they had long since been banned from the city centre by the Roman authorities by the time she came as a pilgrim, back in Jesus' day the Jews had dominated the city (though they were subject to the Roman governor, Pontius Pilate). The centre of their authority – and of the Jewish faith – was the Second Temple. The First had been built by David's son, Solomon, on Mount Moriah, the spot where, according to Jewish tradition, God had created Adam and Eve, and where the biblical patriarch Abraham had prepared to sacrifice his son, Isaac. It had housed the Ark of the Covenant, an elaborate chest containing the two stone tablets on which were written the Ten Commandments, handed down by God to Moses, physical evidence that the Jews were God's chosen people.

Despite that divine protection, the temple had been laid to waste in 597 BCE by the Babylonian King Nebuchadnezzar, who defeated the Jews and carried them off into exile. After their return from captivity in 538 BCE, a Second Temple was built, but without the now lost Ark. And so the Temple remained the focus of Jewish pilgrimage, especially at the three great pilgrimage festivals of Passover (Pesach), Pentecost (Shavuot) and Tabernacles (Sukkot). As instructed in the Hebrew Scriptures, on these occasions Jews would make their way as pilgrims from all corners of the land of Israel, and beyond, to join in festivities and ritual worship at the Temple. On the road, it is said, they would prepare themselves for their destination by reciting the 'Songs of Ascent', sometimes called the 'Pilgrim Songs', and today found in the Book of Psalms. 'Let us go where He is waiting,' reads Psalm 132, 'and worship at His footstool'.

It was the presence of so many pilgrims from far-flung parts that caused moneylenders to gather outside the Second Temple to service the needs of out-of-town folk there for the feast of Passover. The visitors needed to exchange money to pay Temple taxes and buy sacrificial lambs as part of the long-established rituals. These were the merchants who Jesus, in one of the most vivid passages of the Christian gospels, drove out of the Temple precincts, overturning their tables. Alongside the physical and spiritual challenges of pilgrimage, the financial aspect goes right back to its roots.

A Jewish uprising in 70 CE against Roman rule failed, and saw this replacement Temple reduced to ashes like its predecessor. When once more the Jews rose to assert their independence, in 132 CE in the Bar Kokhba revolt, the Romans celebrated victory by adding insult to injury among the vanquished. They placed their own shrine on the Temple Mount to the worship of Jupiter. With the Temple gone, Jewish pilgrims no longer had a focus to travel towards as pilgrims in their yearning for God. Some of the rituals that had surrounded the great pilgrimage festivals that traditionally took place there were domesticated. By the fourth century, however, others were being re-enacted in front of a last remaining fragment of the ruined temple.

Alongside those first Christian pilgrims, then, Jews would gather in the Old City at what had been an outer, supporting wall of the temple. Saint Jerome, who moved to the Holy Land in 385 CE, hoping to be inspired in his translation of the Bible into Latin by living close to the places that feature in its narratives, pictured the scene (and in the process revealed the depth of Christian anti-Semitism). 'You see a sad people coming to visit, decrepit little women and old men encumbered with rags and years ... They weep over the ruins of the Temple. And yet they are not worthy of pity.' Where this arch promoter of Christian pilgrimages to Jerusalem led, later Christian visitors would follow. The sight of the mournful vigils of pious Jews in front of the remnant of their lost patrimony prompted them, scathingly, to dub it the Wailing Wall.

There had been plans to build a Third Temple, but with the Jews no longer having any sort of control over the city that was also their spiritual home, these failed to materialize. So the Western Wall (in Hebrew *Ha-Kotel Ha-Ma'aravi*) became by default the holiest place of prayer and pilgrimage for Jews. And that deep-rooted religious urge to make a pilgrimage to Jerusalem remained strong among the wider Jewish diaspora. Though it waxed and waned over the following centuries, it eventually grew, especially after the establishment of the state of Israel following the Second World War, to become something simultaneously religious and political.

In medieval times, amid one of the periodic upturns in Jewish pilgrimage, it found its clearest expression in a Hebrew poem, 'My Heart is in the East', written by the physician, writer and philosopher Yehuda Halevi around 1141, when he was living in Muslim-controlled Spain.

My heart is in the east, and I in the uttermost west –
How can I find savour in food? How shall it be sweet to me?
How shall I render my vows and my bonds, while yet
Zion lieth beneath the fetter of Edom, and I in Arab chains?
A light thing would it seem to me to leave all the good things
    of Spain –
Seeing how precious in mine eyes to behold the dust of the
    desolate sanctuary.

The heavenly Jerusalem, Zion, and its earthly manifestation combine for the pilgrim into something at once aspirational and real. The broader context of the poem reflects that dual aspect. Despite the reference to 'chains', Halevi lived in what is sometimes referred to as a 'golden age' of Jewish culture in the largely tolerant climate of Spain, or Al-Andalus, under its Muslim rulers. But Halevi was aware – and his words suggest his fellow Sephardic Jews in Spain and Portugal were, too – of a growing threat to that tolerance, both in the age of Christian Crusades, waved off by the Pope to reclaim Jerusalem from its then Muslim rulers, as the place of Jesus' death and resurrection for the Church, and from Catholicism in Spain (seen with good reason as intolerant of the Jews) pushing back against Muslim Al-Andalus in the Iberian Peninsula.

In old age, and increasingly religious after living a more secular life up to that point, Halevi finally went on the pilgrimage he had extolled so powerfully, though it turned out (perhaps by design) to be a one-way trip. He sailed from Spain to Alexandria in Egypt, made his way to Jerusalem, and died there – some accounts say he was trampled by a horse in an accident, others that he was stabbed to death by an Arab at the Western Wall.

Pilgrimage for Halevi had become a return home. In his philosophical writings, notably *Kuzari*, he had argued that true religious fulfilment – which he defined as getting as close as possible to 'the God of Israel' – could only be achieved by Jews physically being in 'the land of Israel'. It is a reference to the key notion of places of pilgrimage having a special spirit that draws people to them. That same mix of spiritual and political imperatives is seen too, in the late nineteenth and early twentieth centuries, when another influx of Jewish pilgrims headed to Jerusalem, escaping the Russian pogroms, and again settled there, fuelling the growing Zionist movement that ultimately resulted in the modern state of Israel.

Today, located at the centre of Jerusalem, regarded by Jews as the capital of Israel (though not by most foreign governments), the Western Wall continues to attract large numbers of visitors. Of the three million people who come to the city each year, 69 per cent go to the Western Wall – a similar number to the Church of the Holy Sepulchre. For Jews, though, it has a special and specific significance. They wedge slips of paper, upon which prayers and petitions to God are written, into the cracks between the stones. The sacred status of this section of large, pale, weather-beaten blocks, together extending to nearly 50 metres long and almost 20 metres high, has been reinforced down the centuries by rabbinical teaching that 'the divine Presence never departs from the Western Wall'. It is an echo of the earlier conviction that the divine Presence was located in the First Temple on the lid of the Ark, between two golden towering cherubim.

※

Such is the extraordinary and compelling geography of Jerusalem that the Western Wall, the holiest place in Judaism, stands cheek by jowl with the golden dome of the Al-Aqsa Sanctuary. In 638 CE, following Allah's first revelation to his Prophet, Muhammad, and as part of the rapid spread of Islam outwards from Mecca into the Near East, Africa and Europe, Jerusalem had been conquered and absorbed into the Islamic Caliphate.

According to the Qur'an, Allah had 'made his servant [Muhammad] travel by night from the sacred place of worship [Mecca] to the furthest place of worship [Jerusalem].'[3] Al-Aqsa, in Arabic, means 'furthest'. This journey, in the Islamic tradition, consists of two parts: the *Isara*, when the Prophet is carried in a dream from Mecca to Jerusalem; and the *Mi'raj*, when he goes from earthly Jerusalem to the heavens. In stage one, he rides to Jerusalem on a mystical white-winged creature, Buraq. Before embarking on stage two, in the company of the Angel Jibril (Gabriel), he leaves his steed behind on the Temple Mount. The Al-Aqsa Mosque is reputedly the exact spot where Buraq waited patiently for Muhammad's return.

It was built by the Muslim rulers of Jerusalem in the late seventh century. Once again, though, what current visitors see – a vast rectangular building – only came later. Like so much of Jerusalem, the original was lost, and the present version was started in 1033 after earthquakes and conflict had destroyed its various predecessors. Alongside this building – typical of early Islamic architecture and still incorporating features that are almost 1,000 years old – is the octagonal Dome of the Rock or *Masjid Al-Sakhrah*. It is, by contrast, more typical of Byzantine architecture – reflecting the strong ties at various stages of its history between Jerusalem, Orthodox Christianity and the centre of that branch of faith in Byzantium/Constantinople/Istanbul. The Dome of the Rock is an Islamic shrine, also dating back to the end of the seventh century. Its vast dome dominates the city's skyline, more so than ever since 1959 when its blackened lead outer skin was covered in gold leaf.

It is the mosque, however, with a capacity of 5,000, that is the third holiest site in Islam – after the Ka'bah in Mecca and the

Prophet's burial place in Medina – and gives the city of Jerusalem special significance for Muslim pilgrims. A prayer in the Al-Aqsa is said to be worth 500 prayers in any other mosque than Mecca and Medina. In Islamic tradition, so important is this site that Muhammad led prayers facing towards Jerusalem in the period straight after his first revelation, until Allah directed him to turn instead towards the Ka'bah in Mecca – symbolically breaking the link with Judeo-Christianity, which had been present in Arabia, and establishing Islam as a religion in its own right.

Despite their separate identities, then, the juxtaposition of major Jewish and Muslim shrines in Jerusalem, with a third, the Church of the Holy Sepulchre at such close quarters through the cramped streets of the Old City, makes the place more than an irresistible pilgrimage destination. It has repeatedly been a flashpoint in the febrile political, cultural and religious conflict for control of the city that stretches from those Babylonian invaders in the sixth century BCE through the various (some of them successful) attempts by Christian Crusaders in the Middle Ages to install themselves as its rulers, right up to the Israeli-Palestinian/Jewish-Muslim stand-off of today. Past and present tensions and bloodshed merge to make a place of pilgrimage into a place of danger – a combination that some medieval Christian pilgrims, believing themselves under God's protection as they travelled thousands of kilometres there on foot through inhospitable terrain, found irresistible.

❈

Empress Helena proved to be a trendsetter, inspiring others to follow in her footsteps and make the pilgrimage from Europe to Jerusalem. Among them, in the 680s, was a French monk, Arculf. On his return journey, his ship was blown off course and he washed

1 The body of Saint James being taken to Spain, painted by the Master of Raigern, *c.* 1425.

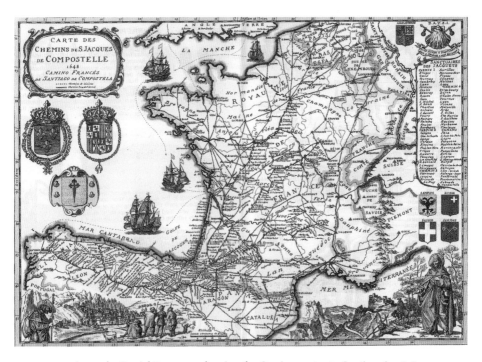

2 A map by Daniel Derveaux showing the Camino routes to Santiago in 1648.

3 Cathedral of Saint James, Santiago de Compostela.

4 The Dome of the Rock and the Western Wall, Jerusalem.

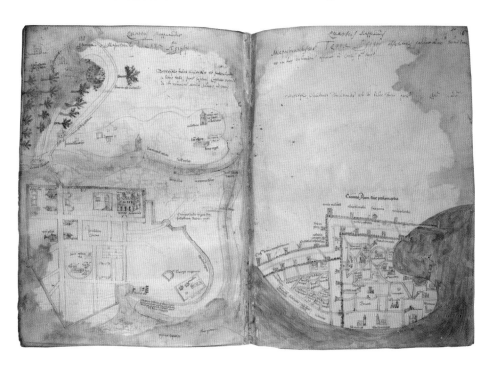

5 The plan of Jerusalem (left) by Pietro Vesconte from *c.* 1320–25 shows the biblical city. The homes ('domus') of King Solomon, Pontius Pilate and Saint Anne and the sites of the Holy Sepulchre ('sepulchrum domini') and the Temple are indicated. The map on the right is of Acre, which fell to Islam in 1290, depicted as a Christian stronghold.

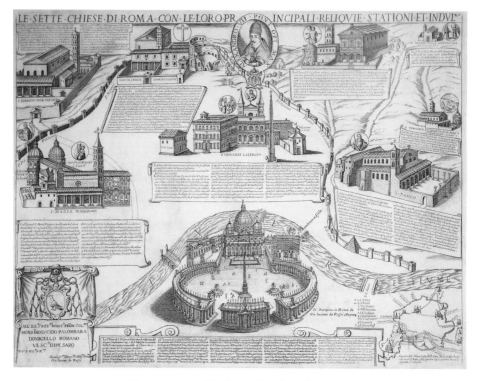

6 Giacomo Lauro, *The Seven Churches of Rome*, 1599.

7 Saint Peter's, Rome.

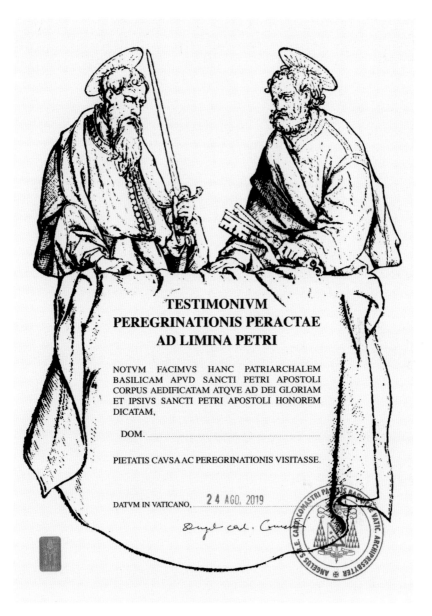

TESTIMONIVM
PEREGRINATIONIS PERACTAE
AD LIMINA PETRI

NOTVM FACIMVS HANC PATRIARCHALEM
BASILICAM APVD SANCTI PETRI APOSTOLI
CORPVS AEDIFICATAM ATQVE AD DEI GLORIAM
ET IPSIVS SANCTI PETRI APOSTOLI HONOREM
DICATAM,

DOM. ....

PIETATIS CAVSA AC PEREGRINATIONIS VISITASSE.

DATVM IN VATICANO, _24 AGO, 2019_

8 The testimonium issued to pilgrims who complete at least
100 kilometres on the path to Rome.

9 The Prophet's tomb in Medina (left) and the Ka'bah in Mecca (right),
from a Collection of Prayers, Morocco, 16th century.

10 Muslim pilgrims doing *tawaf* around the Ka'bah
in Mecca during *hajj*.

11 The rock-cut church of Bet Giyorgis (House of Saint George), Lalibela, Ethiopia.

12 Marija Pavlović (left), one of the original visionaries, prays in Saint James's Church, Medjugorje, 15 August 1987.

13 The Grotto of Our Lady of Lourdes with crutches left behind
by pilgrims amassed on the walls, *c.* 1870.

14 The Abbey ruins on Bardsey Island, North Wales.

up in Scotland, where he recounted in great detail what he had seen to the monk Adomnan, who in turn wrote it all down in *De locis sanctis* (*On Sacred Places*). Copies spread widely all over Europe in the following centuries, adding to what was said in the gospels to confirm Jerusalem's status as the ultimate destination for those wanting to be close to Jesus. Among those who repeated the words used by Arculf via Adomnan was the Venerable Bede, a monk in Jarrow in the northeast of England, in 731 in his *Ecclesiastical History of the English People*.

'For those entering the city of Jerusalem from the northern side,' Bede quotes Arculf as reporting, 'the lay-out of the streets makes the Church of Constantine, known as the Martyrdom [and now as the Church of the Holy Sepulchre], the first of the Holy Places to be visited. This was erected by the Emperor Constantine in magnificent regal style, for this is the place where his mother Helena discovered the Cross of our Lord.[4]

There is mention, too, of a 'lofty, circular' church on the Mount of Olives, just beyond the eastern walls of the Old City today, standing above what has been a Jewish cemetery for 3,000 years. This is where, Arculf states without qualification, 'our Lord ascended into heaven [the risen Christ ascended into heaven forty days after emerging from his tomb, according to the Acts of the Apostles]. In the centre of the Church can be seen his last footprints, exposed to the sky above.'[5]

Such reports – and many others in similar vein – gave, and continue to give, Christian pilgrims to Jerusalem the sensation of being within touching distance of Jesus. So much so, in the early days, that it could tip them over the edge into a kind of hysteria. Some witnesses tell of those first generations of pilgrims in the Church of the Holy Sepulchre trying to bite off chunks of the fragments of the True Cross when they reached the front of the queue waiting patiently to be allowed to kiss it in an act of reverence. Special guards had to be put in place. And Saint Jerome was again on hand to provide a pithy description of pilgrims at the Empty Tomb, kissing it, 'like a thirsty man who had waited long and at last comes to water'. His stated preference was that pilgrims should 'not merely come to Jerusalem but live a holy life there'.

In practice, though, the emphasis in Jerusalem has long been on its capacity to provide a kind of proof to reinforce faith in the names that appear on the pilgrims' itineraries of places to be seen. This is best exemplified by the Empty Tomb in the present-day Church of the Holy Sepulchre. To see it requires waiting in line (at designated hours set by the authorities) before entering an ornate, enclosed shrine, known as the Edicule, then standing in front of the spot where the body of Jesus is said once to have lain before he rose from the dead. In the eyes of the devout, this sight is taken as demonstrating that Jesus *must* have risen from the dead because, otherwise, the tomb wouldn't be empty.

For many contemporary visitors, such a deduction represents too great a leap of faith. It could, after all, simply be a tomb vacated by someone else. Indeed, tests on the marble slabs that make it up – carried out during a 2016 renovation – date them back no further than 345 CE. In other words, it is a symbol of Christian beliefs, not evidence of their accuracy.

Since the Scientific Revolution of the seventeenth century, we have developed a high bar for truth – namely something that can be put under a microscope and shown incontrovertibly to be exactly what it is claimed to be. Many pilgrim sites, though, continue to stand as a sign of contradiction to that modern orthodoxy. They speak to an older variety of truth. It is part of their continuing appeal. Their stories chime with the emotions and intuitions of an earlier age of belief. That is not to patronize those medieval pilgrims who once travelled over land to see at first hand the Holy Places of Jerusalem. They were not stupid, or foolishly credulous, despite the word medieval now being employed as a dismissive adjective. They were, instead, able – in a way that most in the modern age can no longer manage – to hold on to two sorts of truth simultaneously, the physical and the metaphysical: what something is, and the enduring power of the belief that had been invested in it by all those who had walked the same pilgrim route before. For what the empty tomb at the heart of the Church of the Holy Sepulchre represented – and still on some level does – is God's promise that death would not be the end. And that, however scientifically savvy we have become, continues to resonate.

The same logic can be applied to many of the other holy sites in Jerusalem, sacred to all three faiths. Bible scholars may carry on disputing the exact connection claimed between various real-life places and events chronicled in the gospels, just as scientists will point out that Muhammad may have dreamt of coming to Jerusalem, but that doesn't mean he did. Yet for pilgrims it is not the point.

❋

Those who followed in Helena's footsteps did not necessarily have her unlimited access to funds to arrange ships to carry her there and back in comfort. Instead, there quickly developed a tradition of relying instead on their legs, and walking the whole way, with only short stretches of the trek covered by boat. In the Middle Ages, such travellers were known as 'palmers', on account of the Holy Land palm leaf they often sported as they passed through towns, cities and villages across Europe on their long journey home. The souvenir would be either attached whole to their walking staffs or folded into a cross shape (like the crosses that are now distributed in churches on Palm Sunday) and pinned to the hats that protected them from the sun.

Another popular outward sign of the inner grace to be obtained by going on pilgrimage to Jerusalem came in the form of a tattoo. As early as the sixth century, the Christian writer and teacher Procopius, based at the celebrated school of religious thinkers at Gaza, reports in surviving letters encountering passing pilgrims en route home from Jerusalem 110 kilometres to the east, and sporting small crosses tattooed on their wrist as a record of their visit. It is a habit that has lived on. In Jerusalem, today, the Razzouk family parlour, near the Jaffa Gate, claims to have been in business since the 1300s, providing its pilgrim customers with a simple Greek cross (in which all four arms are of equal length) inked on their wrists.

Before getting their palm or their tattoo, however, those pilgrims who flocked across Christian Europe to Jerusalem needed an established route to get there, through often daunting territory. There was no single agreed path to traverse the approximately 5,000 kilometres from the English Channel. Various options rose and fell in popularity over the centuries, depending on what was going on in the countries they passed through. The conversion to Christianity of Duke Geysa in Hungary in 985, for instance, and the subsequent crowning of his son Stephen as the Christian king of the country in 1000, made it easier for pilgrims to travel safely along the river Danube. Stephen even opened pilgrim hostels to encourage the practice.

In general, though, the various paths to Jerusalem tended to fall into three broad categories: those by land across France, over the Alps and down through Italy via Rome to the southern Italian ports of Apulia on the Adriatic coast, where boats left for the Holy Land; those on foot across France and Germany, then down along the eastern coast of the Adriatic through the Balkans to link in with the second century BCE Roman Via Egnatia, later the main trading route through modern-day Albania, Macedonia and Greece to Istanbul, thence either by boat or on foot to Jerusalem; and those again heading through France and Germany on foot but then following various paths through the Danube Valley and cutting across to Istanbul, known as the Via Diagonalis (and sometimes called the Way of Charlemagne – based on a purely fictional visit to Jerusalem that early medieval legend attributed to the first Holy Roman Emperor).

Even during the period of the Crusades, from the end of the eleventh to the end of the thirteenth centuries, there was no single pilgrim road to Jerusalem for those soldiers setting out to return the Holy Land to Christian control. Pope Urban II in 1095 at the Council of Clermont had issued an appeal over the heads of reluctant Catholic monarchs around Europe for an army to gather to liberate Jerusalem and its holy places, which had been under Muslim control since 636. Though the city's Islamic rulers had a long history of tolerance of Christians there, both as residents and pilgrims, tensions had increased in more recent years, with a spate of violent attacks by brigands on caravans of Christian pilgrims making their way from Jaffa on the eastern Mediterranean coast towards Jerusalem. The authorities in Jerusalem were regarded in Europe as guilty of turning a blind eye to such fleecing of pilgrims – and even of benefiting by a cut of the profits.

That, at least, was one practical reason given for taking action, but the real motives behind the Crusades were more much complicated. What Urban was launching was a revolutionary mishmash of pilgrimage, holy war and nod to millennial fever. Urban wanted to deflect discontent with the status quo among the ruled and oppressed of Europe into a holy war to claim back the birthplace of Christianity that he believed would act as a rallying cry to all levels of society. In particular, he hoped it would play on the millennial beliefs found in popular movements of the time that the Second Coming of Christ was imminent, and would take place in Jerusalem, from whence he had departed more or less a thousand years before.

And then Urban added a sweetener: those who fought the good fight to take back Jerusalem and prepare the way for the Saviour would, he decreed, be undertaking a form of atonement for their earthly sins. It was the same idea that was inspiring pilgrims to set out on foot to the early medieval shrines of Europe, such as Walsingham in England where Mary was reported to have appeared in 1061, namely to win remission for their sins and improve their prospects of heaven rather than hell. It was also encouraging believers to visit abbeys, monasteries and churches that contained the holy relics of renowned saints. As a reward for the effort in walking there, and praying before the relics (as well as contributing a few coffers to the plate), there could be a grant of indulgence – a promise that sins committed would be wiped from the slate and entry into heaven made easier.

The Crusades were on an altogether grander, geopolitical scale, requiring those who volunteered to participate to take up arms and kill their enemies to access heaven. 'If any man sets out to free the Church of God at Jerusalem out of pure devotion and not out of love for glory and gain,' Urban promised, summoning all his claimed authority as God's representative on earth, 'the journey shall be accounted a complete penance on his part.'

What is known to history as the First Crusade (there were six more major ones, and a host of minor versions) thereby both militarized and greatly upped the officially offered incentive to go on pilgrimage. Among those attracted was Duke Godfrey of Bouillon, who set out from his ancestral lands in Lorraine 1096 with a ragtag force of 40,000 men. He rejected the route to Jerusalem through Rome, thereby foregoing a papal send-off, and instead headed along the Via Diagonalis. There were to be many trials on the way, especially in the shape of unexpectedly stiff resistance from the Muslim rulers of first Antioch and then Jerusalem, but the Crusaders' eventual triumph-against-all-the-conventional-odds on the battlefield was universally taken as a sign of God's blessing on the whole enterprise.

When Godfrey successfully captured Jerusalem for Christianity in 1099, its Muslim population was promised safety if they gathered in the Al-Aqsa Mosque, but instead were slaughtered. Yet – and in this he is indicative of the religious motives that co-existed (awkwardly to our eyes) alongside bloodthirsty actions in these pilgrim-Crusaders – Godfrey declined the ultimate prize of being crowned King of Jerusalem in the Church of the Holy Sepulchre. He could never, he protested 'wear a crown of gold when my saviour [Jesus] wore a crown of thorns'.

Instead he preferred to be known simply as protector of the city. And that is how he went to his grave. The following year Godfrey died capturing Acre so it could serve as the Crusader port on the Mediterranean coast. The Christian rulers who followed him, including his brother Baldwin, tried to embed and legitimize their rule by lavishing attention on the holy places of their faith in Jerusalem, while at the same time vandalizing those of Jews and Muslims.

By the middle of the thirteenth century, European pilgrims to the city reported (gleefully, in some cases) that only a handful of Jewish families were still living there. The Crusaders had given the Dome of the Rock to Augustinian friars to convert into a church. The Al-Aqsa became for much of the twelfth century the home to the newly founded Knights Templar – traces of the Templar Hall can still be seen as a reminder of the building's contested past on the south wall.

The Templars, named after the two Jewish temples that had once stood on the spot, quickly gained papal approval as a Catholic religious and military order. For many of the Crusaders, once victory had been achieved, their pilgrimage was effectively over, especially when the hoped-for Second Coming did not materialize. As they headed home, it was the Templars, dressed in distinctive white belted mantles with a red cross, who took over the role of protecting the estimated 30,000 Christian pilgrims a year now arriving in the city.

The connection between Godfrey's victory and the founding of the Templars (nine of the original members had been his colleagues) has led some in recent times to label as the Templar Trail the route across Europe to Jerusalem that he is believed to have taken. Though the Templars became a feared fighting force and drew many recruits from Europe, the power they exerted, not just in the Holy Land but subsequently also in Rome and the wider European Church, quickly made them controversial, if not notorious. Their claim to be simply pious pilgrims like those they protected was fatally undermined by the reputation they gained for conspiracy, connivance and ruthlessness on the field of battle, as well as in Church machinations.

They were not ultimately formidable enough, though, to save the whole Crusader enterprise from collapse, which came in 1291 with the defeat in Syria of the last Christian kingdom in the region. The fight to drive back Islam, protect Jerusalem and its pilgrims, and buttress the Orthodox rulers in Constantinople had failed. Muslim overlords regained control of Jerusalem, returning the Dome of the Rock and the Al-Aqsa to their original use, and seizing some

Christian churches as revenge (Saint Anne's, reputedly the birth-place of the Virgin Mary's mother, became a madrassa). As time passed, however, they showed again a general tolerance towards Christian and Jewish pilgrims. The revenue they brought in was judged too valuable to lose.

❁

Modern-day visitors to Jerusalem arrive not on foot or by boat but instead by plane at Tel Aviv and then take a bus. Destination is all, and the journey something to be accomplished as swiftly and effortlessly as possible. Yet a tiny handful still opt to walk the old medieval road, now less travelled, across Europe, in the enduring belief that how you get there is just as important as what you do and see when you arrive. Celebrated among their ranks in recent times is the Scottish Jesuit and spiritual writer Gerard Hughes, an indefatigable do-it-the-hard-way pilgrim who produced two highly popular books on his exertions – *In Search of a Way* (1986) about his trek to Rome, and *Walk to Jerusalem* (1991).[6] The latter described how, after crossing the North Sea from Hull on England's east coast to Rotterdam in Holland, he set out solo, pulling an adapted pram he called Mungo, containing his few belongings, on a pilgrimage via some of the time-honoured routes through Germany, Austria and what was then Yugoslavia to Greece. There he boarded a boat to the Israeli port of Haifa to complete the last leg on foot via Naza-reth to Jerusalem.

Hughes – who died in 2014 – was, in many ways, typical of a certain category of modern pilgrim, rooted in institutional religion but never constrained by it, forever looking for ways on his journey to answer the big questions (in his case the quest for nuclear disarmament and peace) that no papal pronouncement or *Penny*

Catechism formula could provide. A self-confessed 'bewildered, confused and disillusioned Christian', he had what he described as 'a love-hate relationship with the Church', and he relished the opportunity on his pilgrimage to Jerusalem to reflect on and record for his readers his doubts.

Another modern pilgrim walker from England to Jerusalem, Guy Stagg, is perhaps more typical of the newer generation of seekers. He had given up the obligatory Anglican practices of his private school in Britain when he went to university, along with religious faith itself. But in 2013, at the age of 25, he had suffered a breakdown and attempted suicide. He had sought help from mental health professionals but was still left feeling 'unmoored': 'I was looking for a way out, out of my job, out of my life.'

For reasons he couldn't at the time explain, as he recounts in an award-winning book, *The Crossway*, pilgrimage appealed to him as a potential 'way out'.[7] His first attempt was to walk on Chaucer's Canterbury pilgrim route across southern England. Once at the Kent coast, and finding himself feeling marginally better, Stagg decided to carry on, crossing the English Channel and taking the ancient Via Francigena pilgrim path over the Alps to Rome. From there he crossed the Adriatic, picking up the Via Ergenita and onwards to Jerusalem.

Though he had begun with no sense of religious purpose, Stagg found himself, he wrote, being 'drawn upward'. There is, it seems, some residual spiritual power in these centuries-old pilgrim routes across Europe that can pique the curiosity of one whose previous experience of religion had been to 'sing the hymns and zone out during the sermon' as a schoolboy. Staying overnight at some of the churches, convents and hostels that had, for centuries, offered travellers a place to rest their weary limbs, Stagg accepted out of politeness the open welcome they offered to join in their forms of worship.

I didn't understand until then that religious ritual can be nour-
ishing, independent of whether you believe. Or that there is such
a thing as an interior life, and that there are practices that allow
you to explore and expand that life, and that what happens in
that interior life can be reflected in your external life. It makes
people kinder, more benign. I didn't know there was that dimen-
sion to human experience.[8]

Human experience – or spiritual experience? Perhaps it doesn't
matter. The net effect was that he ended his trek in Jerusalem
feeling better. Not cured, but more firmly moored.

For both Hughes and Stagg, Jerusalem itself came as something of an anticlimax, journey's end paled next to the journey
itself. For Jews who come to Jerusalem today, the experience
is different. It is inextricably mixed in with visiting Israel, the
Jewish homeland created in the wake of the Holocaust. Notions
of pilgrimage continue as a result to evolve, but what remains for
a small minority of Jews is the belief that to die and be buried in
Jerusalem is to be in the best possible position to rise again when
the Messiah returns.

The Jewish cemetery on the Mount of Olives, one of the largest
in Judaism, dates back 3,000 years to the time of the First Temple,
when the dead would be buried there in caves, in the shadow of
the Temple Mount. The current graveyard was established around
the sixteenth century and continues to be sought after because
of the tradition that, at the end of days, the Messiah will appear
on the Mount of Olives and make his way to the Temple, giving
the signal for the resurrection of the dead from under the ground
where he walks. For those who cannot make the journey in life,
or in death, soil from there is put into bags and sent off to Jewish
communities around the world to spread on their graves.

For Muslims, too, there remains an attachment to Jerusalem. The story of Muhammad and Buraq is part of their childhood education in the faith but, though it is the third holiest site in Islam, it lags a long way behind Mecca and Medina as a pilgrimage destination, a far cry from the early decades of the eleventh century when records still exist of 20,000 Muslims assembling annually at the Al-Aqsa Sanctuary instead of making the *Hajj* to Mecca. The practical difficulties today in entering Israel from Muslim countries is an added disincentive.

And for Christians? Of the three faiths with competing claims, it is the one that has ruled Jerusalem for the shortest period in its history, yet it provides the most pilgrims today. While the Al-Aqsa is now eclipsed by Mecca and Medina, and for Jews the creation of the state of Israel in 1948 has added new dimensions to the importance of Jerusalem, for Christians in this city of three faiths the appeal of pilgrimage there – the chance to see the Holy Places and walk in Jesus' footsteps – has neither changed nor diminished substantially over the centuries.

CHAPTER 3

ROME
SEEING IS BELIEVING

⁂

*'We are astonished by the discovery ... that our heartstrings have
mysteriously attached themselves to the Eternal City, and are
drawing us thitherward again, as if it were more familiar, more
intimately our home, than even the spot where we were born.'*

NATHANIEL HAWTHORNE, AMERICAN NOVELIST, IN ROME IN 1860

For the weary, footsore pilgrim, catching sight of their final destination is quite a moment. When Martin Luther, then a young
Catholic friar at the end of a 750-kilometre walk over the Alps
from Germany, glimpsed Rome on the far horizon in 1511, he threw
himself to the ground and offered up a prayer of thanksgiving to
God, *'salve, santa Roma'* ('Hail, holy Rome').[1] His gratitude did not,
however, last long once within the city walls, where he had official
business for his Augustinian order in the capital of Catholicism.
Michelangelo may have been at work on the Sistine Chapel and
Raphael in the Vatican, as part of a great Renaissance building
boom, but for Luther the city was not the shrine of holiness and
inspiration that he had been expecting, but instead a den of corruption, vice and degradation.

'I had not been in Rome very long before I had seen much that made me shudder.'[2] His pilgrimage became one more staging point on the road that led to the Reformation he was to precipitate a few years later.

For countless other pilgrims, though, it has the opposite effect, bolstering their faith and making them feel part of something bigger than themselves. Almost four centuries after Luther, the celebrated Anglo-French writer, parliamentarian and controversialist, Hilaire Belloc, arrived on the outskirts of Rome and had exactly the opposite reaction to that of the Protestant reformer. In *The Path to Rome*, a 1902 account of his long walk through eastern France and down the boot of Italy, Belloc recorded being initially deeply disappointed as he reached the outskirts. 'At the foot of the hill I prepared to enter the city, and I lifted up my heart. There was an open space; a tramway: a tram upon it about to be drawn by two lean and tired horses whom in the heat many flies disturbed. There was dust on everything around.'[3] The Dome of Saint Peter's, he complained, 'looked like something newly built'.

Yet once this august pilgrim had stepped through the Aurelian Walls into the vast Piazza del Popolo, his faith was immediately boosted. 'Many churches were to hand; I took the most immediate, which stood just within the wall and was called Our Lady of the People [Santa Maria del Popolo]. Inside were many fine pictures, not in the niminy-piminy manner, but strong, full-coloured, and just.' Mass was ending, but he felt contented enough to sit down and wait twenty minutes for the next one to begin, 'as a pilgrimage cannot be said to be over till the first Mass is heard in Rome'.

For some devout present-day pilgrims – a fraction of the twenty-five million visitors who are estimated to have come to Rome by road, rail and air in 2000 to mark the Holy Year at the start of the new millennium – mass is often the start, not the end of their journey.[4] For many others of more fragile faith, or none at all, mass may not even figure on their itineraries, then or today. Or, if it does, only as a kind of Roman spectacle. Religion may be intimately bound up with the history of Rome as the headquarters of global Catholicism and home to its head, the Pope (who is also Bishop of Rome), but the new generation of pilgrims are content to enjoy the historical and cultural treasures to be found in its churches, as Belloc did, without bothering to wait twenty minutes for the service.

In that regard, as a devout cradle Catholic, Belloc may belong to another age. Yet one reason why *The Path to Rome* has continued to be read ever since publication is that its mixture of travel-writing, history, humour and art appreciation (including Belloc's own drawings made en route) side-by-side with theological musings continues to speak to pilgrims. As Robert Speaight remarked in his authoritative 1957 biography of Belloc, *The Path to Rome* is 'born of something far deeper than the physical experience it records'.

The route Belloc took to Rome was – like much of his writing – idiosyncratic. He followed no established path. Had he done so, he would surely have taken the Via Francigena (literally 'the road that comes from France'), an ancient pilgrim route linking Canterbury and Rome, taken by kings coming and going on the Crusades or wanting to pay homage to the Pope, as well as archbishops, abbots, armies, traders and millions of pilgrims. North to south, it passed through France via Calais, Arras, Reims and Besançon, over the Alps on the Saint Bernard Pass into Italy, and then down through Valle d'Aosta, Pavia, Lucca, Siena and on to Rome. It is thought to have existed in some form since the eighth century, but the first pilgrim traveller ever to record an account of its twists and turns is heard at the end of the tenth century. Sigeric the Serious had been appointed Archbishop of Canterbury in 990 and so headed on foot for Rome to collect in person from Pope John XV his pallium, the liturgical vestment that symbolized his episcopal authority.

In the centuries that followed, the Via Francigena grew and grew in popularity with pilgrims and traders alike. By Belloc's time, however, much of it had fallen into such disuse that it may not even have occurred to him as a practical possibility. And when his great-grandson, the writer Louis Jebb, decided in 1983 to retrace Belloc's footsteps to Rome, he noted that the Via Francigena was known, at that time, only to historians. The original had largely lost its way among the asphalt roads, railroads and hiking trails that bear the modern world hither and thither.

Almost four decades on, it is experiencing a resurrection. There has been official encouragement and support from the Council of Europe, which in 1994 declared it a 'Cultural Route', and from a European Association of the Vie Francigene founded in 2001 (the plural being used because there are some variations on what was originally set down by Sigeric as the authorized version of the route). The Association markets the path to walkers, cyclists and pilgrims alike as 'the journey of life', a means of challenging yourself to cross half a continent while taking in the history of Europe along the way. Behind this revival, all are agreed, lies the huge success (and consequent economic benefits) of the Camino in reinventing itself. Often the Via Francigena is branded as 'the Camino to Rome'. And, like the Camino, there is an office at Saint Peter's where walkers can present their pilgrim passport, if they have done a minimum of 100 kilometres, and obtain not a 'compostela' but a 'testimonium'.

Take-up so far has been modest in comparison to what has been achieved in Spain. Figures are hard to collect since the pilgrim infrastructure around the Via Francigena Nuova remains slight, but

2,500 were recorded as taking the roughly three months required to walk the whole way from France throughout 2012.[5] Most who do it carry a tent, though a new generation of *spedali* – the word a corruption of *ospedali*, meaning hospital or hospice, and the equivalent of *refugios* – has started to crop up in monastic and religious houses on the Italian leg of the journey, where signage is also rapidly improving. There is, as yet, little of the buzz of conviviality and shared experience that surrounds the Camino. As a way of getting to Rome, the Via Francigena remains the choice of less than 1 per cent of visitors.

For some of a solitary disposition, that is one of its advantages. In 2010, 60-year-old Brian Mooney, a long-serving Reuters correspondent in Rome, set out from Saint Paul's Cathedral in London for Saint Peter's Basilica following the Via Francigena on a trek that took him seventy-six days. In his published account, he recorded with approval that he had experienced none of 'the hullabaloo of the crowded Camino'.[6] Others have recognized, though, that the Via Francigena does share with its Spanish cousin an appeal to the twenty-first-century pilgrim, curious, keen on a challenge, but largely un-churched. 'The boy behind the bar in Cavaglia asked me for my "motive",' writes retired architect Christopher Lambert of his time on the route in 2000 in his illustrated account, *Taking a Line for a Walk.*[7]

> *I felt a charlatan when I answered 'Pellegrino' [pilgrim]. I had travelled under the protection which this word still provides. I had 'used' it to gain entry and shelter to and from monasteries. I had said a prayer to the Almighty in the hope that he would forgive me those trespasses. I was carrying my pilgrim's 'passport', but at heart I was a pale imitation of those millions who had travelled this route over hundreds of years. If Doubting*

[apostle] Thomas had qualified to walk this way, then fine;
a questioning but hopeful point of view might exonerate my
hypocrisy.

❁

Christian tradition holds that Rome – as the centre of the empire
that ruled Jerusalem at the time of Jesus – was the focus of the
Church from its very inception. Both Saint Peter, chosen by Jesus
according to the gospels as his 'rock',[8] and Saint Paul, the most per-
suasive of those missionaries who shaped and spread the new faith,
are said to have been put to death in the imperial capital around
67 CE. Historians question the truth of such claims,[9] but there was
certainly an early flow of Christian mourners, who over time were
perhaps better described as pilgrims, at what was reputed to be the
grave of Peter in the city at the Vatican necropolis, a 2,000-year-
old burial ground for Romans. In the second and third centuries
CE, the grave – mixed in among those of pagan Romans – took on
a more formal shape as a pillared memorial, and saw even more
Christians coming to stand in front of it. In the fourth century, as
part of the vast building programme that followed Christianity
becoming the official religion of the empire, the whole necropolis
area on the Vatican Hill was flattened and covered by a basilica
named after Peter. Because it was over his grave, it was claimed as
the mother church of Christianity (rather than the Church of the
Holy Sepulchre, on the spot where Jesus died).

Pilgrims eager to immerse themselves in this early history of
the Church can today visit what remains of the graveyard as part
of a tour underneath present-day Saint Peter's of the excavations
('*scavi*' in Italian) conducted in the middle years of the last century.
It circles round the unearthed tombs, as the feet of visitors to the

basilica echo above, and culminates behind and below the main altar in the basilica where the tour comes back up to almost ground level in what is called the *Campus Petri*, or 'Field of Peter'. Behind a glass wall stands a section of the original white grave pillars, held up by brickwork that has been dated back to 150 CE. Alongside is a fragment of a 'graffiti wall', where those early-days pilgrims would scratch prayers to the first pope when they came to the original necropolis to visit his then open-air grave. The only just-about legible one, written in Greek, reads: *'Petros eni'* or 'Peter is here'.

In 1950, the space was opened to public view, the first time in 1,500 years that physical evidence was accessible to pilgrims of the long-standing Church claim that the basilica stood on the place of Peter's burial. In those early years of showing them to the public, the claims made for the bone fragments, on display behind the glass, were nuanced. They *might* be Peter's, was as far as it went. In the late 1960s some of them, found in a niche in the Graffiti Wall, were examined by archaeologists and pronounced to be those of a man, aged between 60 and 70, who had died in the first century CE. That fitted the bare facts about Peter, but what clinched it – as far as the Church authorities were concerned, and the devout Catholic pilgrims who visit today – was that no bone fragments had been found that came from below the ankles. The popular story has always been that Peter insisted on being crucified upside down, feeling himself unworthy to die in the same way as his Lord. When his corpse was cut down from the cross, it was suggested, the guards would have chopped it off below where the ankles were nailed in place, and thus handed over Peter's footless body to his followers for burial. It falls short of scientific proof, but that does nothing to stem the tide of pilgrims arriving through the basilica at this spot, where they join the few who have been on the Scavi tour. On pilgrimage, seeing is believing.

There was, as already seen, turmoil in Europe in the centuries after Charlemagne that served as to deter pilgrims from the north. Instead of taking to the main routes to Rome, with their real or imagined dangers, they headed off instead on the reputedly less risky Camino. This caused a decline in Rome's status as Christian Europe's pilgrim destination of choice. The Jubilee or Holy Year of 1300 was an attempt by Pope Boniface VIII to win back lost business. On this special occasion, he decreed, those who braved the journey to Rome would be rewarded with a 'plenary indulgence', a promise endorsed by the Church and set out on a sheet of parchment handed out (for a fee) at Saint Peter's. It declared that, on account of their hard slog in walking to Rome to celebrate the jubilee, the bearer's sins had been forgiven. In some forms it even allowed the living, by their pilgrim efforts, to reduce the time their deceased loved ones would have to spend in the anteroom of purgatory before being admitted into heaven.

Boniface's initiative grew out of what had long been a practice in Catholicism – for those monks and higher clergy who had committed particularly heinous crimes to be sent, by way of penance, to walk to Rome to confess their sins to the Pope in person. Only his absolution would cleanse their souls, and it required proof of their contrition in the form of the distance they had covered on foot. Yet the plenary indulgences of the Jubilee Year of 1300 were not about demonstrating penance to the Pope, but rather pilgrims receiving what was effectively a free pass into heaven as a reward for their efforts in travelling so far. Controversially, the Pope was making money out of dispensing God's justice on His behalf.

Whatever the ethics of the offer, many found it irresistible, and pilgrim numbers climbed steeply as Jubilee years quickly became a feature of the calendar in Rome, declared at regular intervals. And, more widely, the sale of indulgences spread, with no requirement for those who bought them to travel as pilgrims to Rome. Such abuses contributed to Martin Luther's attack on the Catholic Church that led to the Reformation in the early sixteenth century. He had been scandalized, while on his own 1511 pilgrimage to Rome, that the revenue generated from indulgences had been used by Julius II (1503–13) to fund his rebuilding of Rome on a sumptuous scale.

For his part, Julius tried to argue that his efforts would make Rome ever more a magnet for future generations of pilgrims. In other words, he was saying that it was a virtuous circle of investing in upgrading churches and basilicas to attract pilgrims and hence increase revenue so as to invest more. Powerful voices, notably the Dutch priest and theologian Desiderius Erasmus, who lived in Rome from 1506 to 1509, ridiculed such flawed logic. In his satire *Julius Excluded from Heaven*, Erasmus pictures Julius II arriving at the gates of paradise and boasting to the doorkeeper, Saint Peter, of his achievements: 'I raised revenue, I invented new offices and sold them ... I have covered Rome with palaces and I have left five millions in the treasury behind me.'[10]

Peter was not impressed, according to Erasmus, but today's generation of visitors – without necessarily knowing it – are grateful for the buildings commissioned by Julius and his successors. Many of the churches, palazzos, basilicas and art works that are must-see stops on any pilgrim route around Rome date back to this period.

❁

If walking all the way across Europe is regarded as a step too far by most modern pilgrims to Rome, then the city itself all but requires its visitors to get footsore. Its *centro storico* (historic centre) is compact, easily manageable by pedestrians, and too narrow for coaches. Private cars have been all but shut out of its maze of cobbled streets, punctuated by wide squares. And even 'outlying' locations, such as the Vatican on the other side of the river Tiber (since 1929 and a treaty between the Catholic Church and the Italian dictator Mussolini, it has the status of a mini sovereign state of just 44 hectares), are within striking distance for walkers. The home of the popes lies across the Ponte Sant'Angelo, lined with attendant life-size sculptures of angels. From there, the most popular pilgrim route in the whole city leads up the Via della Conciliazione, bull-dozed in the 1930s through the old Borgo, to the vast, colonnaded piazza (by the genius Bernini) in front of Saint Peter's.

There are, though, many other pathways around the city, each with layer after layer of pilgrim associations stretching back 1,600 years, and in some cases beyond, to pre-Christian times. The best known of these long-established routes links what are known as the Seven Pilgrim Churches of Rome. The tradition began in Holy Week of 1552, as Christianity prepared for its greatest annual feast of Easter, when the Florentine preacher Filippo Neri, later Saint Philip Neri, led a group of followers on a 19-kilometre, day-long pilgrimage round the great churches of the city. He intended it as a counterpoint to the more bawdy carnival that was taking place on the same day. Neri gathered his party at the tomb of Saint Peter for prayers, and then they set off to visit in turn Saint Paul's Outside-the-Walls (which contains the tomb of the apostle Paul), Saint Sebastian's, Saint John Lateran, Santa Croce-in-Jerusalem (built to house the relics of Jesus' death brought back from the Holy Land by the Empress Helena), Saint Lawrence Outside-the-Walls and finally what is called in English Saint Mary Major, but which sounds so much better in Italian as the fourth-century basilica of Santa Maria Maggiore.

Four of the seven – Saint Peter's, Saint Paul's, Saint John Lateran and Santa Maria Maggiore – are, in church terms, deemed to be 'major' basilicas (hence the name of the last one), and therefore, in Jubilee years, pilgrims could gain an extra indulgence by walking through their 'Holy Doors', entrances that are kept sealed for the rest of the time and only opened to mark these high points on the pilgrim calendar. The symbolism – every ritual act in Catholicism carries a heavy weight of symbolism – is that the pilgrim, as they pass through the Porta Sancta (Holy Door) goes from the everyday world into the presence of God. As is written in John's gospel, where Jesus promises, 'I am the gate. Whoever enters through me will be saved.'[11] It is the essence of Christian pilgrimage compressed into an action that takes just a few seconds.

In that first Jubilee Year of 1300, the Holy Door indulgence applied only to Saint Peter's, but in 1500 it was expanded to the other three as well. Their opening – breaking the seals that held them firmly shut – itself became a ritual that drew crowds, with the fragments of shattered mortar that fell to the floor gathered and prized as sacred relics.

As a guide, Filippo Neri knew all too well about meeting the needs and hopes of pilgrims to the city, having earlier in 1548 founded the Confraternity of the Most Holy Trinity of Pilgrims and Convalescents, dedicated to caring for the thousands of poor, pious travellers who had walked long distances to Rome for yet another Jubilee year that had been declared. His agenda went further. Sometimes referred to by his admirers as the 'third apostle' of Rome – after Peter and Paul – Neri was a significant figure in the Counter-Reformation, and the Seven Pilgrim Churches route was one among many ways in which he and others strove to restore reverence and probity to the spiritual life of the city, and by association Catholicism, after both had come under sustained and wounding attack as godless ever since Luther had launched the Reformation in 1517. His new brand of Protestantism had won many converts among God-fearing folk, especially in northern Europe, and had therefore caused a decline in pilgrim numbers in Rome itself.

As well as refocusing and cleansing Catholicism, Neri also realized that – whatever Luther's attacks on the practice of selling them – indulgences still had great appeal, especially when built in as an incentive to go on pilgrimage. The very first Jubilee Year in 1300 had encouraged the faithful to come to Rome by granting indulgences. The offer had covered Saint Peter's Basilica and Saint Paul's Outside-the-Walls, in particular, since most visitors were drawn especially by the prospect of standing next to the last remains, and relics, of the two founding apostles of their Church. Now, with the Seven Churches walk, that could be broadened. There was an indulgence for those who processed round all seven. Especially prized was to do the walk in Holy Week, as the printed guidebooks that started appearing in the sixteenth century made plain. In a 1585 edition, Antoine Lafréry included a map of the seven, and told those who followed it that if they stayed in Rome for a year and attended mass at Saint Paul's each Sunday, they would have completed the equivalent of a full pilgrimage to Jerusalem or Santiago de Compostela. Pilgrimage was a competitive business, then as now, for those who depended on the revenues it raised. Rome had to establish a practical – if not spiritual – precedence in pilgrim eyes over its Spanish and Holy Land rivals.

The Seven Churches route circles the centre of Rome, but as part of the Renaissance rebuilding spree of the fifteenth and sixteenth centuries, pilgrim pathways also played a significant part in urban planning and reordering in the heart of the city. Rome was adapting itself to become more attractive to the legions of pilgrims who made their way through the centre from all directions towards the Vatican. A Via Peregrinorum developed, with existing streets joined up, widened, and lined by churches, palaces and goldsmiths – selling their goods to visitors. And to accommodate those popes who enjoyed parading through the streets of 'their' city, carrying relics of the saints with them that were usually on display in churches, a wide pathway was cleared from the Vatican to the basilica of Saint John Lateran, the cathedral church of the diocese of Rome.

Today's Via del Pellegrino, leading down from the flower market in the Campo de' Fiori towards the Tiber, with Saint Peter's on the other bank, is the only section of the medieval Via Peregrinorum to reference its earlier purpose. But dotted around the city are numerous reminders of what in the past drew pilgrims. The current English College in Via di Monserrato, for example, has been a seminary for training Catholic priests since 1579. It stands on the site of the English Pilgrims' Hostel (or Hospice, as it was called) that was established in 1362 in a property purchased from a seller of rosary beads. It had been founded to provide a safe place for those who had walked all the way to Rome from Canterbury and beyond. For the Jubilee Year of 1450, it is recorded that it accommodated 1,022 pilgrims over the course of twelve months, part of the influx of 40,000 drawn to Rome by that release of promises of indulgences.[12] Many would stay not for days or weeks, but rather months, which was judged to be the recuperation period required before undertaking the return journey on foot. It was for most a once-in-a-lifetime experience.

And then there is the wayside shrine or *edicola* that today stands small and forlorn on the route between the Vatican and Lateran, next to the twelfth-century Church of Santi Quattro Coronati. It is said to mark the spot where in the ninth century, Papessa Giovanna, or Pope Joan, a woman who had disguised herself as a man to claim the papacy, gave birth in the street and was – along with her baby – stoned to death by an angry crowd. The Church has long denied that there is any truth in the story, but in medieval times the site in question was widely known to pilgrims as the Vicus Papissa – 'the small street of the woman pope'. The *Mirabilia Urbis Romae (Marvels of the City of Rome)*, the most popular of the sixteenth-century printed pilgrim guidebooks, draws its readers' attention to a statue of the female pope 'nigh unto the Colosseum'.[13] Floral tributes would be placed there, and prayers said, whatever the objections of priests and bishops. Pilgrimage, history shows, cannot be easily regulated around a single set of officially approved stories.

There was a different sort of pilgrim in evidence in Rome from the second half of the seventeenth century through to early decades of the nineteenth century. With the Treaty of Münster of 1648 bringing to an end the Thirty Years War and restoring peace to those parts of Europe crossed by time-honoured north-south pilgrim routes, the 'Grand Tour' was born. Young men, and later women, from well-heeled families, often accompanied by an older chaperone, descended on the city to immerse themselves for months, sometimes years, in the art, culture and philosophy to be found in such abundance in the place that gave birth to Western civilization. If asked, such visitors, initially mainly from Protestant Britain, though their numbers subsequently were swollen by wealthy new arrivals from North and South America, would most likely have described this coming-of-age ritual as 'educational'. Yet part of the education they sought, Rome being what Rome is, involved at the very least observing religion, and usually attending services, if not participating fully in them.

An early nineteenth-century chronicler of life in the city noted that, at the Easter Sunday high mass at Saint Peter's, 'three fourths of the crowd was British'.[14] The Vatican, though, was growing tired of the detachment of Grand Tourers who attended Church liturgies. Throughout the 1820s, it issued warnings against treating its masses as a 'fashionable promenade'. Some reports spoke of the tourists eating sandwiches and popping champagne corks during lengthy major services, as if at an outdoor opera or concert.[15] It was, arguably, an earlier version of the sort of behaviour that still sees Roman churches and basilicas putting up notices asking present-day pilgrims to keep their voices down and their clothing modest so as not to distract genuine worshippers.

It illustrates how the same tensions keep cropping up down the ages around pilgrimage, principal among them the pull and push between it being a penitential exercise to cleanse souls and win grace, or something fun and mind-expanding. It is as much there in Chaucer's *Canterbury Tales* in the fourteenth century as it is for twenty-first-century *peregrinos*, and nowhere more so than in Rome today, where it is almost impossible to separate out the religious from the historical, the clerical from the classical. The modern visitor, with Rome now Europe's third most-popular destination after London and Paris, is more likely to be a non-believer than a devout Catholic. In contrast to those who came in earlier centuries, they are able to jet in and out for a long weekend, with little of the physical effort or once-in-a-lifetime commitment common to both medieval pilgrims and Grand Tourers. Yet, curiously but somehow inevitably, these contemporary pilgrims still end up filling their time by going into churches or heading for the city's most popular site (with 4.2 million visitors annually), the Vatican Museum. Essential to any tour of the treasure trove in its miles of galleries is reaching the Sistine Chapel, where necks are strained to peer in awe at Michelangelo's account of Jesus Christ dispensing the Last Judgment on humankind for its sins.

Perhaps the real draw of Rome, then, is that it is a place where the secular and the religious co-exist in a real, tangible and enjoyable way. On its streets the invisible – the spiritual side that remains strong, even in an age where formal religious attachments have loosened or been discarded – is made visible, in churches, basilicas and shrines, and in the footsteps left behind, unseen but present, of the generations of pilgrims who have come before. Lord Byron – not an obviously pious or devout individual – recognized it when, in 1818 in his autobiographical poem *Childe Harold's Pilgrimage*, he extolled the power of the Roman catacombs, the vast underground vaults of the dead on the outskirts of the city. In its early centuries, Christianity's persecuted faithful had gathered in these tunnels and caves to celebrate services that fortified their refusal to recant, even unto death, what they believed to be the truth.

> *The Roman saw these tombs in his own age,*
> *These Sepulchres of Cities, which excite*
> *Sad wonder, and his yet surviving page*
> *The moral lesson bears, drawn from such pilgrimage*

CHAPTER 4

MECCA
A WORLD APART

✲

'Our notions of Mecca must be drawn from the Arabians; as no unbeliever is permitted to enter the city, our travellers are silent.'

EDWARD GIBBON, *THE HISTORY OF THE DECLINE AND FALL OF THE ROMAN EMPIRE* (1776–89)

A mecca draws people to it because it does what it does better than anywhere else. The expression was first used in English in this way in the nineteenth century. An 1826 article in the doctors' journal *The Lancet* describes the medical schools of Scotland as 'a mecca for the studious'. Nowadays it is readily and repeatedly applied to anything from shopping malls to ski slopes and surfer beaches. The origin is, of course, Mecca, the holiest city in Islam, visited each year by up to four million pilgrims, but while its name has been widely appropriated, Mecca itself is not a mecca for all modern-day pilgrims. Entry remains, as it has been since the earliest days of Islam in the seventh century CE, restricted only to Muslims. The new generation of unaffiliated pilgrims, for now, is not welcome.

One of the very few non-Muslims to have experienced Mecca during *hajj*, the high point of its year, was the British traveller Sir

Richard Burton in 1853. Back then, there were none of the visa controls and checkpoints into the city that currently filter out non-Muslim pilgrims, so with the unstoppable curiosity of the Victorian explorer determined to 'open up' the world, he set out to circumvent what barriers did exist. He was resolved, he wrote, on 'removing the opprobrium to modern adventure, the huge white blot which in our maps still notes the Eastern and Central regions of Arabia'.[1]

Burton slipped unnoticed into Mecca by donning a disguise that allowed him to blend in with a party of visiting Pathans, Afghan Muslims, whom he had first encountered and befriended when serving as a British army officer in India. He had journeyed overland with them, in the traditional manner of pilgrims, with the Egyptian capital Cairo as a major gathering point. Some Muslims who congregated there would have walked all the way from the west coast of Africa, taking several years and living as they journeyed as nomads. Burton's group then crossed Sinai, where they joined others travelling from points further north on the *darb-al-hajj,* the principal route that heads south through the Arabian Desert to, first, Medina (where the Prophet Muhammad is buried) and then Mecca. Tracing its origins as far back as the Iron Age, this road had been established in the fourth century BCE for trading and religious reasons by the Nabatean kings (they, too, regarded Mecca as a holy place, and worshipped their deities there). It was then upgraded by the all-conquering Romans, who renamed it the Via Nova Triana. In the early years of the sixteenth century, with the expansion of the Ottoman Empire to include Mecca, it continued to be a major artery for officials, armies, merchants and the pilgrimages that were waved off with great ceremony from Constantinople for *hajj.* And fifty years after Burton, it provided the template for the Hijaz Railway, which reached as far as Medina, when the outbreak of the First World War prevented the completion of the last leg to Mecca.

Burton's account of Mecca, published in 1855,[2] complete with sketches and maps, quickly became the classic commentary in the English-speaking world in the second half of the nineteenth century on Muslim life and manners. For all his gung-ho chutzpah about allowing no door to be closed in his face, he was careful in print to issue a stern warning to anyone tempted to follow in his footsteps.

> At the pilgrimage season disguise is easy on account of the vast and varied multitudes which visit Mecca... But woe to the unfortunate who happens to be recognized in public as an Infidel... Amidst a crowd of pilgrims, whose fanaticism is worked up to the highest pitch, detection would probably ensure his dismissal at once. Those who find danger the salt of pleasure may visit Mecca; but if asked whether the results justify the risk, I should reply in the negative.[3]

Whether that was a verdict on Mecca itself, or a belated realization of the insult his deception had visited on Islam, Burton doesn't make plain. What does come across loud and clear, however, is just how intrigued and even seduced he had been by what he witnessed once inside the forbidden city during the traditional five days of *hajj*. This is one of the five pillars of Islam, the essential practices that all Muslims must carry out if they have their health and sufficient money to do so. Burton provides graphic first-hand descriptions of being amid chaotic crowds of pilgrims circling seven times round the Ka'bah, intent on 'besieging' the cube-shaped shrine that represents the presence of Allah at the very centre of the Grand Mosque. As he took his leave of Mecca, Burton reflects not on the thrill of having got away with his audacious mission, but on the profound impact that the place has made on those around him.

> *A general plunge into worldly pursuits and pleasures announced the end of the pilgrimage ceremonies. All the devotees were now whitewashed, the book of their sins was a tabula rasa: too many of them lost no time in ... opening a fresh account. The faith must not bear the blame of the irregularities. They may be equally observed in the Calvinist, after a Sunday of prayer, sinning through Monday with a zest, and the Romanist falling back with new fervour upon the causes of his confession and penance, as in the Muslim who washes his soul clean by running and circumambulation; and, in fairness, it must be observed that ... in the Muslim persuasion, there are many notable exceptions to this rule of extremes. Several of my friends and acquaintances date their reformation from their first sight of the Kaabah.*[4]

Such is the undiminished power of Mecca in our own otherwise very different times that there is an unmissable echo of Burton in the verdict delivered 150 years later by a contemporary visitor to Mecca, the popular British television presenter Jason Mohammad. Raised a Muslim by his Pakistani father in Cardiff, he recorded a documentary in 2009 about his own first pilgrimage to Mecca that afforded rare first-hand insights for non-Muslims by a familiar guide into what it is like inside the city. He had travelled outside *hajj* season – which comes once a year in *Dhu-al-Hijjah*, the twelfth and final month in the Islamic lunar calendar. Instead his visit was an *'umrah*, or 'lesser pilgrimage' to Mecca, recommended by Islam as something to be done at any time of the year, but not a religious obligation like *hajj*. Standing in front of the Ka'bah had been, according to Jason Mohammad, a milestone in his life. 'It changed me as a person. People say they cannot explain what it feels like to stand there, and I had never understood. Now I have been, I do understand. I was overtaken by the same feelings. You are at peace and the rest of the world doesn't exist.'[5]

All pilgrimage sites have, to some extent, the capacity to evoke a sense of stepping outside the everyday world and gaining a new perspective. In Mecca, though, this takes a distinctive turn precisely because the city is restricted to the 1.5 billion Muslims around the globe. First and last this is a place that is about responding to a specific instruction in the Qur'an. 'Proclaim the Pilgrimage to all people. They will come to you on foot and on every kind of lean camel, emerging from every deep mountain pass, to attain benefits and mention God's name, on specified days.'[6]

Yet there is more to it than that. Here in Mecca for those who come on *hajj* or *'umrah* from all corners of the world – some of them countries with majority Muslim populations, others where Muslims are a small minority – one of the core tenets of their faith is made tangible. The essential and special brotherhood (and sisterhood) between fellow believers is lived out daily, as the black American civil rights activist and Muslim convert Malcolm X recorded in his account of *hajj* in April 1964.

Muslims [are] here of all colors and from every part of this earth. During the past days here in Mecca, while understanding the rituals of the hajj, I have eaten from the same plate, drank from the same glass, and slept on the same bed or rug – with kings, potentates and other forms of rulers – with fellow Muslims whose skin was the whitest of white, whose eyes was the bluest of blue, and whose hair was the blondest of blond. I could look into their blue eyes and see that they regarded me as the same, because their faith in One God [Allah] had actually removed 'white' from their mind, which automatically changed their attitude and their behavior [towards] people of other colors.[7]

On his return to the States Malcolm X put the prefix El-Hajj before his name – as all who complete *hajj* are entitled to do – and was known thereafter as El-Hajj Malik El-Shabazz, and began to argue that mainstream Islam offered a way forward in tackling the racial tensions in the United States. Ten months later he was assassinated.

❁

In 570, Mecca was the birthplace of the Prophet Muhammad. As well as its trading prowess in the centre of the Hijaz region of the Arabian Peninsula, it already had a lengthy history as a holy place, the discovery there many centuries before in such an arid region of an underground water source, the Zamzam Well, giving it a reputation for being touched by the miraculous. At the very heart of the city, and of equal antiquity to the well, was the Ka'bah, which archaeologists speculate may have once housed within its stone walls the sacred utensils of the Zamzam cult. In this inner sanctuary of Mecca, long before Muhammad's times, once a year, pilgrims from far beyond the city would come on what they called *hajj*.

Trade and religion were inextricably linked in Mecca. Its ruling tribe, the Quraysh, believed that the presence of the Ka'bah was responsible for their economic prosperity. As did others, who envied their good fortune. In the late 540s, the rulers of Yemen, further south, part of the Christian Aksum kingdom in Ethiopia that lay across the Red Sea, had gone so far as to establish a rival shrine in Sana'a, and then launch an attack on Mecca to disprove its claim that it was somehow divinely protected. The strategy backfired spectacularly, when the elephants at the head of their army reached the outskirts of Mecca, and reportedly promptly fell to their knees in reverence at the holiness of the Ka'bah. The creatures refused to take one more step forward. 'The Year of the Elephant', which coincided with Muhammad's birth, confirmed Meccans in their sense of spiritual superiority.

Feeling better than others did not, however, bring harmony to the city's population. These divisions troubled Muhammad, a respected and upright member of the ruling tribe, who had been orphaned in early childhood, but as an adult had become a merchant who, in 595, had married Khadijah, herself a successful businesswoman and fifteen years his senior. In 610, he left behind his wife and children and retreated to a cave 3 kilometres outside the city on Mount Hira to pray for guidance. Here he was visited by the Angel Jibril – Arabic for Gabriel, already well-known in the Jewish and Christian traditions – and heard the first words of a new Arabic scripture pouring, as if unbidden, from his lips. Islam was born, and with it a development of the rituals that already existed in Mecca.

The story behind *hajj* became about Muhammad, notably about how, in March 632, his health visibly failing, he led the pilgrimage, bequeathing firm instructions in his farewell sermon on Mount Arafat as to how Muslims must treat each other not as rivals but as brothers – 'know that every Muslim is a Muslim's brother, and that the Muslims are brethren. It is only lawful to take from a brother what he gives you willingly, so wrong not yourselves'.[8] He was precise about the ways in which, henceforth, *hajj* should be performed. These incorporated traditional rituals around the well of Zamzam and the Ka'bah – in the same way that expanding Christianity in Europe had built upon, refocused and effectively subsumed existing pagan sites – but also provided a new understanding of them that was part of the framework of Islam. This eliminated many of the practices, especially around the Ka'bah, that had in the past caused controversy, with Meccans charging visitors to go inside the building (today it is closed during *hajj* because of the sheer weight of numbers) where a statue of Hubal, a moon deity, was worshipped. On his return to Mecca in 630 from exile in Medina, one of Muhammad's first acts was to smash the idol to Hubal.

Key to his new cleansed version of how things were to be in future with just one god was to fashion a new narrative of the past. Muhammad re-explained how the Zamzam Well and the Ka'bah had first come to be in Mecca, and thereby made the most significant human figure in *hajj* not himself but Ibrahim (Abraham). This biblical patriarch is as central to Islam as he is to Judaism and Christianity. In Mecca, Muhammad taught, Muslims were walking in the footprints of Ibrahim.

In Jewish and Christian texts, Hagar, an Egyptian servant girl, has a son with Abraham, with the blessing of Abraham's childless wife, Sarah. However, after God's intervention, Sarah (in her 80s) conceives Isaac, a child of her own with Abraham. She turns against Hagar and her son, Ishmael, and insists that her husband banish them to the desert. God tells Abraham to go along with this demand but promises that he will make Ishmael 'into a nation'.[9]

In Islam, this promise comes to life. Ibrahim brings his wife Hajar (Hagar) and their son Isma'il (Ishmael) to Arabia. In the desert, Ibrahim abandons them, at God's behest, and Hajar is left to run frantically to and fro between two hills in search of water for her baby. That moment is re-enacted on *hajj* in the ritual of *sa'ee*. Pilgrims run seven times – or, more usually, walk briskly – up and down a marble-floored, air-conditioned tented corridor from the steps of al-Safa beside the Ka'bah across to al-Marwah. It joins the two hills in Hajar's story. When she returns empty-handed to her infant, the narrative continues, Hajar finds that Isma'il has been scratching the earth. When she looks more closely, she discovers the underground spring at Zamzam.

It now forms a part of the Grand Mosque complex, but at the epicentre remains the Ka'bah. Pilgrims had already been circling it seven times in the centuries before Muhammad. This structure, he now told his supporters, had been built by Ibrahim, with the help of Isma'il.[10] While it – and the rituals that surrounded it – had been misappropriated subsequently for the worship of pagan deities, now it was to be restored to the worship of the one God, Allah.

And it has been ever since, with new traditions growing up around it. The Persian-born medieval scholar Al-Zamkhshari (died 1144) lived for many years in Mecca, where he was so admired that he became known as 'God's neighbour'. In his writings, he suggested that it was the Angel Jibril who had guided Ibrahim and Isma'il to the spot where the Ka'bah was built, and had even shaded them with his wings from the sun as they went about their labours. Today, a squarish stone on the ground a few metres away from the structure, encased in glass and marked with footprints, is referred to as the 'Station of Ibrahim' and is said to be where he stood while watching over the construction of the Ka'bah.

The angel also provided the father-and-son building team with the black stone that is embedded in the eastern corner of the Ka'bah's walls, the only remaining part of the original structure to survive the floods and fires that have afflicted it over the centuries. It is this stone that pilgrims (including Sir Richard Burton) fight their way through the circling crowds to touch. In the Hadith, a record of the traditions and sayings of the Prophet, it is said that the stone was originally whiter than milk but had been made black by the sins of humankind.

In the years following Muhammad's death, the Islamic caliphate he had inspired spread rapidly and widely, to include under its sovereignty Jerusalem, much of North Africa, and lands as distant as Spain and Persia. This rapid expansion of what was referred to as 'the Abode of Islam' provided a greatly enlarged pool of potential pilgrims, under a religious obligation (if able) to travel to Mecca. And so the caravans on the pilgrim routes increased, the thirty-five-day journey from Cairo, or the thirty from Damascus, as nothing for many who came compared to the long treks by land and sea just to arrive at these starting points. For them *hajj* became a journey of several years.

One factor in the centuries since of unbroken continuity has been that Mecca has always remained a city apart, a holy place, not a political hub. All violence is forbidden there, and though there have been times in its history when it was attacked, in the main it has been left out of conflicts. As the Islamic caliphate spread out from Mecca across the Middle East, into Africa and Europe, it established its political headquarters elsewhere – including Damascus and Baghdad. Yet the authorities upheld Mecca's special status, ruthlessly when required. So when in the late ninth and early tenth centuries the Sufi mystical and esoteric movement in Islam grew strong with its teaching of an inward journey in search of truth, those who sought to downplay the importance of the physical journey of *hajj* were dealt with severely. One of their number, Husain al-Mansur, also known as al-Hallaj, the Wool-Carder, claimed that it was possible to make a valid *hajj* in spirit while staying at home. He was executed in 922.

If some would do down the role of Mecca, others championed alternative sites. On the pilgrim route to Mecca from the north, the path from Baghdad led through Karbala, scene of a decisive battle in October 680 CE in the on-going clash between those factions who claimed the Prophet's authority as leader of the caliphate. Husayn ibn Ali and his brother Abbas, grandsons of Muhammad and sons of the fourth caliph, had refused to pledge allegiance to the new non-family head of the caliphate, Yazid I, arguing that he was not following the teachings of the Prophet. At Karbala they were killed and their claims dashed, but the profound resentment it caused fed into the breach in Islam between Sunnis, who today make up around 80 per cent of Muslims, and Shi'a (15 per cent). While all Muslims regard Mecca and Medina as the most sacred places, the tombs of Husayn and Abbas at Karbala, 100 kilometres southwest of Baghdad, continue to have a special reverence for Shi'a.

It is estimated that anything up to eight million pilgrims come each year – making Karbala the biggest shrine in Islam, ahead of Mecca. Their visits focus on two dates in particular. *Ashura*, on the tenth day of the month of Muharram, the first in the Islamic calendar, marks the anniversary of Husayn's death and is a public holiday in Afghanistan, Bahrain, Iraq, Iran, Lebanon and Pakistan when Shi'a pilgrims flock to Karbala. And then forty days later, *Arba'in* is the biggest event in the year, when the period of mourning based on the teachings of the Prophet comes to an end, and around twenty million people, many on foot, head for Karbala, both to remember those who died in the battle, and to recall and honour their own dead relatives. Unlike Mecca, Karbala does not exclude non-Muslims. Christians, Yazidis, Zoroastrians and other believers from the region can join in.

※

To cross the border – or *miqat* – that surrounds the holy city of Mecca, all four million *hajaj* or pilgrims who arrive each year must be dressed in *ihram* clothing. *Ihram* is less a set of sartorial rules – though that is how it can seem – more a state of mind, which is symbolized by what you wear, a way of each pilgrim opening themselves up, putting worldly concerns to one side, and creating the space to focus more on the soul than the body. What is effectively the uniform for pilgrims – two white sheets for men that contain no seams, knots or stitching, worn with shoes that leave the ankle and back of the foot exposed, and a full-length dress and *khimar*, or head covering, for women – is intended as the outward sign of an inner renunciation of everyday life.

It is simultaneously a reminder, by its shroud-like appearance, that all wearers are equal, whatever is in their bank accounts, and that they are, when in Mecca, somewhere between this world and the next, between this life and eternal life. It is a rehearsal for Judgment Day, which may explain why so many *hajaj* return home with a sense of change and renewal.

Ihram also requires other forms of self-denial over the five days of *hajj* to avoid anyone getting distracted from the main purpose. No perfume should be worn – special unscented soap is available. Men must not cut their nails, hair or beard. Women should not wear make-up. There is to be no swearing, no quarrelling, no fighting and no smoking. Men must refrain from staring at women, and sex, even for married couples, is not permitted. Gender-segregation rules, such as enforced in many mosques, are more relaxed, but it remains difficult for a single Muslim woman under 45 to undertake *hajj* unless accompanied by her father or brother.

How the various days of *hajj* are organized varies from pilgrim to pilgrim. There is a sense that each individual is the spiritual director of their own pilgrimage. Most begin on day one with the *'umrah*, or 'lesser pilgrimage' rituals, which can be performed year-round. There is the circling, seven times, anti-clockwise, around the Ka'bah, which Muslims believe mirrors the movement of angels directly above in heaven who circle the *bait ul ma'mur* ('frequented house') in paradise. Draped in a black silk cloth, or *kiswah*, onto which are embroidered verses from the Qur'an in golden calligraphy, the Ka'bah is the very centre of the lives of every Muslim, the direction in which they must turn to pray five times a day – and another of the five pillars of Islam. With so many people in attendance during *hajj*, and younger men traditionally encouraged to walk at a hurried pace, actually getting to touch, or kiss, the black stone in its walls is nigh on impossible. With admirable pragmatism, visitors are today urged simply to point at it as they recite supplications to Allah. And because, in some matters, Mecca bends to modernity, *hajaj* can now point their selfie sticks at the Ka'bah, with the resulting posts going up on social media and allowing non-Muslims access, albeit virtual, without the deception employed by Sir Richard Burton.

Next stop is the Zamzam Well, where water can be drunk, before undertaking *sa'ee*, the walk backwards and forwards between the two hills, in imitation of Hajar in the desert. Other component parts of *hajj*, which can happen in whatever order suits the pilgrim, include spending the first night of *hajj* in the sprawling tented village in the valley of Mina, outside Mecca, before heading to Mount Arafat, where Muhammad preached his final sermon and set out the rules for *hajj* ever after. Arrival should be by midday, and those who are able spend the hours until sunset standing in prayer and contemplation, often in the blazing heat.

Because the Islamic calendar is based on the moon, each year is ten or eleven days shorter than in a standard calendar, and so the period of *hajj* moves through the seasons over a cycle of years. For those who visit when *hajj* falls in mid-summer, temperatures can rise above 40 centigrade.

After Arafat, at sundown, the pilgrims head for Muzdalifa, to the west, some walking, others taking buses, to collect stones for the next day. After another night under canvas, often in vast male and female dormitories, they head to Jamarat, where they stand on a bridge – a recent addition to the sacred geography of *hajj* – to throw seven of the stones each at the largest of three pillars that represent the devil. This is done in memory of the occasion on which Shaytan (the devil) tried to woo Ibrahim and persuade him not to submit (Islam means 'submission') to God's will.

Next, recalling Ibrahim's willingness to sacrifice his son, *hajaj* are required to slaughter a sheep, goat, cow or camel. What this means in reality for almost all is that they pay a fee for it to be done in their name. At this point, in a traditional pilgrimage, men can shave their hair, women cut a piece of theirs, and all can remove their *ihram* clothes. There follows a second and final '*tawaf*', or seven circuits round the Ka'bah. Prayers are offered in line with the Prophet's words: 'the pilgrim intercedes for 400 of his relatives and is as sinless as on the day his mother gave birth to him'.

Afterwards some may choose to take a trip – not obligatory to complete *hajj* – to Medina to see Muhammad's tomb, returning to Mecca for three more days to join in the festivities for Eid al-Adha, or the festival of sacrifice, celebrated by Muslims around the world to commemorate Ibrahim's test of faith. Livestock is slaughtered and the meat distributed to the poor.

❖

The essential rituals and patterns of *hajj* have remained largely unchanged over the centuries. That thread connects the current generation of visitors to Mecca with past generations all the way back to Muhammad, and even beyond. It is, once again, the walking where others have walked, and the praying as they prayed. Such continuity is crucial to what makes *hajj* a genuine once-in-a-lifetime experience for pilgrims.

The backdrop to *hajj*, however, in the form of the cityscape of Mecca itself, is only of secondary importance. And so, in recent years, it has undergone a rapid and – to some eyes – not wholly sympathetic transformation. Most pilgrim sites around the globe place an exaggerated premium on authenticity, those connections with the past that give the place an authority. Wherever possible, original buildings and overall look are preserved. In Mecca, by contrast, such concerns have come a distant second to the practical task of accommodating 2.3 million visitors who arrive in such a concentrated period of time at *hajj*, and the additional 1.7 million who come at other times of the year for *'umrah*.

Following the collapse of the Ottoman Empire at the end of the First World War, overlordship of Mecca passed in 1925 into the hands of Ibn Saud, founder and first monarch of modern-day Saudi Arabia. His dynastic successors are guardians of the holy city, as once were the caliphs of Damascus, then Baghdad, the sultans of Cairo, and the Ottoman rulers in Constantinople. With the financial resources generated by the large-scale oil production that began to flow in earnest in the Arabian Peninsula in the 1930s, they have built roads and – with the first flight arriving from Cairo in 1937 – airports at Medina and the Red Sea port of Jeddah, 80 kilometres away. The latter is equipped with a special *hajj* terminal, capable of handling fifty incoming planes per hour in peak season. It includes *ihram* rooms where those disembarking can change into the prescribed dress for pilgrims before heading up the Jeddah to Mecca highway and through the spectacular Qur'an Gate, built in 1979 in the shape of a book stand holding the sacred text.

Some other developments have, however, proved controversial. The demolition in 2002 of the Ajyad Fortress, an Ottoman citadel built in the eighteenth century to defend the Grand Mosque which it overlooked, caused an international outcry. It was replaced, once the hill on which it stood had been levelled, by an unmissable, grandiose luxury hotel, topped by a Big Ben-like clock tower that dwarves the Ka'bah. The complex comes complete with a five-storey shopping mall and car parks. It is, though, just the most prominent of many uncompromisingly modern buildings that dominate the Mecca skyline, part of a planned expansion of facilities that has, since 1985, seen the loss of older landmarks in the city associated with the Prophet and his family. These include the house of his uncle, Hamza, flattened by bulldozers in 2014 to make way for another hotel, and the house of Khadijah, his first wife, now virtually obliterated.

The insatiable demand for efficient, functional urban architecture and infrastructure to cater for the crowds at *hajj* and *'umrah* is one obvious driver for the changes. Debated, too, is whether there is also a dislike in play within Wahhabism, the prevailing Saudi strain of Islam, of any exaggerated emphasis on visits to shrines, tombs or religio-historical sites. Too much veneration of relics of the past – in this case the old city of Mecca – could amount to Islam's gravest sin: worshipping anyone or thing other than Allah.

The Saudi government has an entire ministry dedicated to managing Mecca. It is responsible for the visas that all overseas pilgrims must obtain to go to Mecca or Medina (old-style pilgrim taxes were abolished in 1972). These are limited at present for *hajj* by the sheer constraints of space. In 2013, for example, numbers of visas granted were efficiently reduced by a fifth for that year alone to take account of major building works going on. The ministry also dispenses grants to Muslims who otherwise could not afford to make the journey. Three-quarters of *hajj* visas for over-seas pilgrims currently go to just eight countries, of which seven (Indonesia, Pakistan, Bangladesh, Iran, Egypt, Nigeria and Turkey) have Muslim-majority populations.

Managing the influx can stretch resources to breaking point. In 1990 the failure of a ventilation system in a pedestrian tunnel caused a stampede that left 1,426 pilgrims dead, while a similar malfunction in 2015 at Mina cost 700 lives. Neither has modern-day Mecca been immune to the global rise in terrorism. In 1979, a group of armed dissidents seized the Grand Mosque and took hostages. After a two-week siege, soldiers stormed the stronghold, but hundreds of pilgrims were killed in the ensuing battle.

Such tragic episodes are the antithesis of the faith invested in *hajj* by pilgrims and have accelerated the official drive to improve both facilities and security in Mecca. The Grand Mosque – often also referred to as the Al-Haram or Haram Mosque – is growing its current capacity of 1.5 million upwards to a stagger-ing thirty million by 2030, while the *mataf*, the area where the faithful circle the Ka'bah, has been trebled in size to accommo-date 150,000 people at any one time. Such ambitions will mean further changes to the fabric of Mecca, and to at least some of the twenty remaining structures there believed to date back to the time of the Prophet.

Does it matter? The line between tourism and pilgrimage is – as has been seen before in these pages – an almost impossible one to draw. Separate from Mecca, Saudi Arabia announced plans in 2019 to 'open up' the country to foreign tourists. Visas are to be available not just to those wanting to make pilgrimages, but also to those keen to take in other sights in the country. E-visas, it is promised, will take as little as seven minutes to process, while female tourists can expect to be exempted from previous strict dress codes that meant they would have to wear the *abaya*, a garment that covers the body from neck to feet, anywhere in the kingdom.

The tourist push is born of economic necessity. Currently foreign pilgrims account for 3 per cent of national revenues. By 2030, the official aim is to increase that to 10 per cent in order to diversify the economy from reliance on oil exports in the age of climate change. Whether that might one day lead Mecca to be included in the list of sights open to tourists as well as Muslim pilgrims is publicly discussed. 'Selfie' videos by pilgrims are, after all, readily available on the Internet, while in the real world reforms now mean parts of Medina are open to non-Muslims, though not the central sections around the Prophet's tomb. A high-speed railway now links Mecca with Medina, with a 'Light Rail' system in Mecca itself, built and operated by a Chinese company. And pictures even emerged in late 2019 of apparently non-Muslim Chinese visitors being shown round Mecca, in what some see as a foretaste of what the Saudi authorities may be contemplating.

In a place where the essentials of pilgrimage are unchanging, any loosening of rules might bring Mecca in line with other modern-day sites, but its particular identity is bound up in being timeless and different from the rest. Inevitably something precious would be lost.

CHAPTER FIVE

LALIBELA UNEARTHING A MYSTERY

※

'It wearied me to write more of these works because [my readers] will accuse me of untruth.'

<small>PORTUGUESE PRIEST FRANCISCO ALVARES ON 'DISCOVERING' THE CHURCHES AT LALIBELA IN THE 1520S</small>

It is four o'clock in the morning, just as the sun is starting to rise in the thin air of the bleak and beautiful Ethiopian Highlands, 2,500 metres above sea level. Locals join pilgrims who have travelled here from all around the country as they walk steadily and purposefully behind their priests through the red haze that is thrown up by the wheels of the occasional vehicle passing by along the dirt road across this pinkish-red sandstone terrain. Most of the figures passing across this already dramatic landscape are dressed as is the tradition in bleached white cotton ceremonial *natelas*, often from head to foot. Up ahead, there appears to be no particular destination in sight. They are walking, as pilgrims do, in search of something intangible. Then, all of a sudden, the ground in front of the crowd opens up and they start descending into the Lalibela complex.

Some pilgrims journey with their eyes cast upwards in search of a glimpse of heaven. Others, focusing on what is in front of them, seek out paradise on earth. At Lalibela, though, the 100,000 Orthodox Christians who come every year as pilgrims, some trudging over mountains barefoot, invariably have their gazes cast down to catch sight of this particular place of wonder, a group of eleven ancient churches that have been sculpted in the ground. By common consent, the oldest dates back 900 years, constructed by methods that even the scientific might of the twenty-first century still cannot quite fathom. Some have been shaped out of a single slab of stone that is itself contained in a vast pit excavated down into the earth.

The pilgrim procession disappears as if down a sluice as it decants below ground level via tiers of steep steps and a labyrinth of underground tunnels that incorporate grottoes, hermit caves and catacombs, where hermit monks and ascetics live. The churches themselves, though, are open to the air, some of their roofs lining up with the earth's surface. Around them subterranean courtyards are squeezed in between their outer walls and the sides of the gigantic hole in the ground that contains them. But no description on the page can quite prepare pilgrims for their first glimpse of this holy site, where more than any other destination on earth time suddenly has no meaning, where ancient and modern combine as one, and where structures frozen in time and in the earth speak eloquently and mysteriously of the enduring power of belief.

Modern-day Lalibela remains an unusual choice for Western spiritual tourists, but an upgraded airport and decent road into the centre is pushing numbers up. During the great festivals most visitors are still from the forty-million strong Ethiopian Orthodox

Tewahedo Church. They camp out in the cold night air often on nothing more than a plastic groundsheet. The commercialism of hotels, hostels and first-world comforts has yet to overwhelm the town. By day, time-honoured rituals unfurl as they have for centuries. Orthodoxy, in Ethiopia, as in its other branches, takes seriously its claim to be unchanging. It is what draws people to Lalibela.

The eleven churches peep out of their hiding places in three clusters: five to the north of the complex, including both the largest, Bet Medhane Alem (House of the Saviour of the World), and the oldest, Bet Maryam (House of Mary); five to the south, among them Bet Abba Libanos (House of Abbot Libanos), its façade scarred by alarming cracks; and one, Bet Giyorgis (the House of Saint George) nestling down all on its own, the best known and most photographed of them all. From ground level it is certainly the most arresting, with its flat roof shaped to mirror the Greek cross engraved on it. All eleven, though, are as much carvings as architecture. They conform to few of the usual conventions about great religious edifices. They have no ambition to soar to the heavens like the spires of the medieval cathedrals of Europe that are their near contemporaries. And scarcely a brick appears to have been used in their construction.

In the great pits that house them, some of the churches have elaborate façades chiselled into the walls that hold back the earth on the four sides of these subterranean tanks. Others among the eleven, the most striking, emerge not out of the restraining walls but instead stand free and proud in the centre of their hollowed-out precincts. They rise as a single piece of carved stone. Decorated on their outside walls, and around doors and windows, with geometric patterns, inside their darkened, candle-lit, sectioned-off sanctuaries are more lavish, with intricately patterned ceilings that juxtapose the Madonna and Child, a wandering African lion and a dry Acacia tree. Like it, these churches grow out of the ground.

What has kept them alive for nine centuries in what is the only pre-colonial period Christian church in sub-Saharan Africa is the nourishing water of the faith of the pilgrims who have travelled to visit them. The whole of this complex, a man-made version of heaven fashioned out of nature and anchored in and to the earth, positively throbs with religious fervour. For those who prefer the light-touch approach to faith on the Camino, Lalibela might quickly become too much for it floods the senses: the sight of the pilgrims descending the steps; the pungent but somehow reassuring smell of the earth; the omnipresent sound of chanting; and the touch of ancient rock that has witnessed so much history. Their combined power can be overpowering.

The churches may be monumental, but they are not huge. The largest, Mehdane Alem, is just 30 metres in length (Saint Peter's Basilica stretches to 186 metres), the smallest, Bet Denagel (The House of the Virgins), windowless and all but buried in the side of the courtyard of Bet Maryam, is 9 by 8 metres.

✿

In the early morning light, it is to Saint George's – named after the patron saint of Ethiopia's Orthodox Christians, who make up 44 per cent of their country's population – that the procession is heading. Tall, thin, pale and mottled pink and yellow on the outside, it nestles in a square rock container that is 22 by 22 metres (the equivalent of approximately twelve adults lying head to toe) and goes down to a depth of 11 metres (or six adults). Even at this hour of the day, all who come cannot hope to fit inside the church. Not that many want to. Stepping through the doors (shoes must be removed) is something usually reserved for the very old and the very young. The ritual is as much about being outdoors around the building as it is standing next to the altar.

Looking down from above in the pale aurora, the gloom of the narrow, high-walled courtyard is illuminated by the white garments and headgear of the gathering pilgrims. Several prostrate themselves, ritually touching what they regard as holy ground three times with their heads. Others perform a variation where they kiss and touch the fabric of the church. It brings them, they believe, as close to their maker as if they were inside on their knees in prayer.

In that prevailing spirit in Orthodoxy of standing firm against the winds of change that elsewhere have reshaped other churches (Greek Orthodoxy has the same liturgy now as it did in the fourth century), at Lalibela the language employed in all rituals pointedly defies time. Ge'ez ceased to be heard in daily conversation in Ethiopia in the eleventh century, but it remains the only tongue used in these churches. Chanted prayers begin to drift out from inside and float upward on the greyish-blue clouds of incense that stream out of the glassless windows. As they rise, they join one world with the other that begins at ground level. Earthiness and unearthliness merge seamlessly.

The mystery of who built these churches, how it was done, and for what reason, only deepens the faith of pilgrims who come to Lalibela. That no satisfactory explanation has yet been provided embellishes its reputation as a place apart from the world, able to be something beyond everyday concerns and knowledge. It is a quality that links it to other pilgrim sites thousands of kilometres away, such as Stonehenge. There, the 5,000-year-old circle of mighty standing stones on Salisbury Plain in southern England has steadfastly down the centuries resisted all attempts to reveal the secrets of its original purpose and its construction, with the result that its popularity with visitors grows year on year.

Likewise Lalibela. Those who cannot face the walk over the mountains still have to endure a bumpy ten-hour bus journey from the Ethiopian capital, Addis Ababa. Once arrived, they simply embrace the mystery that surrounds the site. There can be no satisfactory earthly answer, their faith teaches them, because this is a sacred place, the handiwork of God. So extreme are the technical challenges that had to be overcome to create the churches, and so inexplicable the decision to turn all wisdom on its head and locate them down into the earth, that they can only be the product of a bigger, better, wiser divine hand. Lalibela's very existence is taken as proof of God's existence. What greater draw can there be for pilgrims?

By most estimates, the churches date back to the late twelfth and early thirteenth centuries. Some scholars, however, notably David Phillipson, have argued that the earliest of the structures could reach back to the seventh or eighth centuries. Yet at the core of the beliefs that animate the place are spiritual roots that go back much further, to a thousand years before Jesus when, as the Old Testament recounts, a 'queen from the south' – usually known as the Queen of Sheba – travelled from Ethiopia to Jerusalem to study under the Jewish king Solomon, son of David, builder of the First Temple, and renowned for his wisdom. This queen is said to have returned to her people from her travels with versions of many of the Hebrew Scriptures and established Judaism in her lands.

Her relationship with the Jewish king was not only spiritual and cerebral. They had a son, Menelik, who went on to found a great dynasty in Ethiopia, based in part on the religion his mother had introduced after her time with Solomon. One story, recounted in the Kebra Nagast ('Glory of the Kings'), among the holiest texts in

Ethiopian Orthodoxy, tells how Menelik also travelled to Jerusalem, to meet his father, and came back with the Ark of the Covenant, which – it is claimed – is housed to this day amid great secrecy in the Church of Our Lady of Zion in Aksum, the ancient Ethiopian capital. Only its monk-guardian is allowed to see it, but over the centuries those few others who have been permitted a peek suggest that it is a replica. Whatever the truth, the legend makes the point that, just as Christianity grew out of Judaism, so too did its Ethiopian Orthodox incarnation.

Among the early Christians, some accounts identify either Matthew, the former tax collector among the apostles, or Matthias – according to the Acts of the Apostles elected after the crucifixion to replace the traitor Judas Iscariot in the ranks of the twelve given the task of spreading Jesus' teaching to all nations – took the Good News to Ethiopia ('the city of cannibals') in the first century CE. Acts also tells of Philip the Evangelist, one of Jesus' disciples, converting an 'Ethiopian' official. In the standard Ethiopian Orthodox narrative, this detail is used to suggest that there existed a pilgrim route between their country and Jerusalem, but biblical scholars now believe that the term 'Ethiopian' was used more loosely to denote anyone with black skin from Africa.

On better but by no means entirely sound historical foundations stands the legend of Frumentius, a Syrian Christian monk – or merchant depending on which version you read – who was shipwrecked in the early years of the fourth century CE and sold into slavery at the court of Ezana, who then ruled over the Aksumite empire in Ethiopia. Among his captors Frumentius began to make converts to Christianity and, when freed, elected to continue his mission in Aksum, afterwards being named Bishop of Ethiopia by the Patriarch of Alexandria, Saint Athanasius the Great. Thanks to Frumentius's successful efforts Christianity became the official religion of Aksum – before Constantine had bestowed the same recognition on it in the Roman Empire, making Ethiopia by some disputed calculations the world's first officially Christian country.

What Frumentius had started, others subsequently carried forward, notably establishing in the fifth and sixth centuries a chain of Christian monasteries, including that at Adwa, which houses the Garima Gospels, believed to be the earliest surviving illuminated (illustrated) Christian manuscripts in the world. When the eastern and western branches of Christianity split in the eleventh century, Ethiopia followed the Orthodox tradition rather than the Pope in Rome. However, while it was in theory under the authority of the Coptic Orthodox Patriarch of Alexandria, its geographical isolation far to the south saw it develop its own distinctive form of worship. Today, an Ethiopian Orthodox Patriarch, based in Addis Ababa, leads what has become a separate and distinctive church, in many ways as far removed from Greek Orthodoxy as it is from Catholicism.

King Lalibela (1181–1221) was part of that Church and of the ruling Zagwe dynasty (the word comes from the Greek for 'land of burned faces') that had supplanted the Aksumite rulers of northern Ethiopia in the tenth century CE. He is said to have been a particularly pious and saintly Orthodox Christian. The Zagwe had migrated their capital further inland as part of a shift in their power base in Ethiopia around 1000 CE, fearing that Aksum itself was too vulnerable to Muslim raids launched from the Red Sea coastline. The new capital was originally known as Roha, but later was given the king's name, Lalibela – which means 'let the bees obey him', a reference to the swarm that is supposed to have appeared at the king's birth, landed on his infant body, but did not sting him.

If King Lalibela appeared chosen by God from the very start, his upbringing was nonetheless a tough and dangerous one in a fractious and fractured royal court. He had to endure the hostility of his uncle, and the machinations of an older half-brother, Harbe, who joined forces with a half-sister on one occasion to slip something nasty enough to kill him into an outwardly enticing drink. The hagiographical story goes that, generous by nature, Lalibela had passed the poisoned chalice to a deacon so he could taste the cocktail prepared by his siblings. The poor man then dropped dead, as did a passing dog who licked him.

Feeling himself unworthy to survive after another had died in his place, the tale continues, Lalibela finished off the dregs in the cup, and collapsed into a deep sleep. In it, he was taken by God to see ten churches carved from a single rock. Three days later, the dregs not being sufficient to finish him off, he rose Christ-like from the dead. Believing himself spared by God for a purpose, he set about recreating the vision of rock churches he had seen.

As with many of the most eye-catching religious narratives, beguiling to the devout among pilgrims, the details do not bear too much scrutiny. More earthbound suggestions for the origins of this place include that Lalibela had travelled to Jerusalem, and held it in great esteem. When Saladin and his Muslim forces subsequently seized the city in 1197, he was devastated and decided to commission a 'New Jerusalem' to which pilgrims could come because they were now unable to access the real thing. Alternatively, a rather more tangible Muslim threat may have been experienced by the Christian rulers of northern Ethiopia, as they faced incursions from across the Red Sea. In such a reading, the churches of Lalibela were intended by their creator as both a digging-in (literally) and a rallying point by and for a particular and distinctive Christian religious culture under siege.

Today's Lalibela certainly carries a superficial echo of the Jerusalem of the gospels. The drainage ditch that runs through it, stopping the pits from filling up, is known as the Jordan, though it is not a river. Yet this complex is no replica, even in the loosest sense. It is all about symbolism that connects it with Jerusalem. Inside Bet Medhane Alem, the grandest of the eleven churches, with a rock-hewn façade more akin to a Greek Temple, and surrounded by thirty-four rectangular columns, there are three empty tombs, waiting for the bodies of Abraham, Isaac and Jacob, the three biblical patriarchs, a resting place in death if Jerusalem itself turns its back on them under a Muslim ruler. Likewise in Bet Golgotha (the Church of Golgotha – where women are forbidden to enter) are tombs for Christ and Adam (alongside one later occupied by King Lalibela).

These are monuments of reference and reverence. There were and remain plenty of other Christian sites in Ethiopia symbolically given names from the Holy Land. In south Gandor, for example, is a Monastery of Bethlehem. In Oromo, is found a Mount of Olives.

More likely, then, that Lalibela was conceived, in part at least, to approximate to the vision of a holy city that the king had seen in his dream when languishing after being poisoned. 'Lalibela set out to create a place where God's presence is found and where the worshipper and pilgrim can travel to enter the holy presence,' writes John Binns in his 2017 history of the Orthodox Church of Ethiopia. Symbolism rather than likeness is all-important, because it teaches pilgrims the basic truths of their faith. That would certainly account for the details of the construction – why, for instance, Bet Maryam stands alongside Bet Mehdane Alem, the church of Jesus' mother next to that of her son, the Saviour of the World.

Symbolism can also be political, however much such earthly concerns today are largely put to one side when pilgrims come here to escape this world. Legend has it that King Lalibela had another dream (such nocturnal reveries also figure large in the

Hebrew Scriptures/Christian Old Testament and in the Qur'an). It took place just as the whole complex of ten churches neared completion. In it the king saw Saint George, Ethiopia's patron, slaying the country's enemies. When he awoke, Lalibela realized he had failed to allocate George a place of his own in the sacred town-planning of his new Jerusalem, and so he commissioned an eleventh church, Bet Giyorgis. In some versions he dies before it is finished and his widow completes the task in his memory.

Again, sheltering behind the pious legend may be a more pragmatic motive. Tying his own name so ostentatiously to the ultimate saintly protector of the Ethiopians would have done King Lalibela's security of tenure as ruler no harm whatsoever. And if you look with a historical rather than pious eye at the Lalibela complex, it is possible to trace another story. Bet Amanuel (The House of Emmanuel – the word that translates as 'God is with us' in Hebrew) may have the finest carvings of all eleven churches, but their original purpose seems to have been to celebrate the king rather than God, since this was originally a royal chapel. Meanwhile Bet Merkorios (The House of Mark the Evangelist) contains ankle shackles that suggest it was a jail for those who opposed the king's rule. Yet in these overlapping layers of history – earthly and divine – Bet Merkorios simultaneously can only be reached by a 35-metre, unlit tunnel from Bet Gabriel-Rufael (The House of the Angels Gabriel and Raphael), a route, as Orthodox pilgrims believe, that is designed to be a foretaste of being in hell.

With the spiritual and the historical so entangled, the central conundrum of Lalibela remains unresolved: how were these buildings actually made, and made so quickly, with nothing a modern builder would recognize as a labour-saving device or an earth-moving tool? And, moreover, made so well in a hostile climate that they still endure today (though some – notably Bet Medhane

Alem and Bet Abba Libanos – have their roofs covered by modern, ugly corrugated iron tarpaulins to keep out the rains and the sun to prevent further decay)? The pilgrims' answer to the conundrum, when the matter is raised is, of course, to say that God built Lalibela. As it has been throughout Lalibela's history. While the labourers slept after a long day's work, states the *Gadla Lalibela*, an Orthodox church hagiography of the king, written soon after his death, angels would come down from heaven to take their place and get on with the work at four times the speed of mere mortals.

Modern archaeologists are, needless to say, unconvinced by such explanations, but they struggle to offer any alternative as to why these churches were buried. Rock-hewn and cave churches, chapels and monasteries, are seen in other parts of northern Ethiopia, with especially fine and spectacular examples further north in Tigray, dating as far back as the sixth century CE, but they are all above ground level – thousands of metres above, in some cases – and usually stand alone. Why, then, at Lalibela, were the churches submerged, and why were there eleven of them in one place, rather than just one?

The two questions may be linked. If you put your church in a pit, it will necessarily be limited in scale by the size of the hole you can dig. A series of pits with mini churches in them might have been the logical solution, the combination of eleven structures together adding up to something the equivalent of a vast cathedral. If that really was the intention, it has failed, for among the pilgrims who go there today, most of the eleven are treated as separate and distinct, and many who visit go only to their particular favourite.

Such a scheme also doesn't address why the king effectively buried the churches. Might it have been for military purposes? But surely they would have been easier to defend in the face of an onslaught by Muslim forces if above ground? Attackers could swarm into a pit faster than they could scale a forbidding outer wall. So could it have been a solution to the particular problems of preserving structures against the climate at such high altitude – effectively putting them in a container where the earth walls would mitigate fluctuations in temperature? Though Ethiopia covers just 4 per cent of the African continent's landmass, it has half of its land over 2,000 metres and 80 per cent of that over 3,000, with all the attendant climate challenges that brings. A local solution, then, to a local problem? It just feels too breathtakingly hard-to-achieve to justify such an undertaking.

And these churches are, it cannot be emphasized enough, no mere primitive sunken shells. They are works of art, their very painstaking details something which further strengthens the argument that they may have been started long before Lalibela's time, and should therefore be viewed as the work of centuries not decades, time enough for human hands to do the hard labour. Their interiors contain an array of different styles – Greek pillars, Arabesque windows, and spectacular wall paintings – while their arrangements imitate those of the Jewish Temple. Bet Maryam, the Church of Our Lady, and one of the most popular with today's pilgrims, contains in its east wall a decorative detail that is believed unknown anywhere else in the world. There are two rows of three windows, fashioned out of the rock. The upper trio represents the Holy Trinity, even more significant in Orthodoxy than in Western Christianity. The lower three sit under a carved cross and thus recreate the hill of Calvary where Jesus died. The central window of the lower three is for him. That to his right is for Dismas, the thief who repented and was promised eternal life in heaven by Jesus. We know that because it includes in its design a small opening above it, to symbolize a glimpse of paradise. That to the left is for Gestas, the criminal who did not ask forgiveness. It accordingly features a small opening below it – a peephole into hell where he will suffer in torment forever.

✿

Lalibela is at its most otherworldly during its peak pilgrim season, which occurs at Christmas. Because the Ethiopian Orthodox Church continues to use the old Julian calendar, rather than the Gregorian one adopted in the West and most other places since 1582, that means it celebrates the birth of Christ not in late December but instead in what is for the rest of the world early January. That also makes it the most popular time for Western pilgrims to come – tacking on a holiday after the festive season with their relatives.

The main event is Timkat (sometimes Temqat), the biggest of the festivals at Lalibela, as it is throughout the Ethiopian Orthodox Church generally. It falls on 19 January on standard calendars (or 20 in a leap year) and combines both the Epiphany – when in Western Christianity the arrival of the three kings at the child Jesus' manger in Bethlehem is marked – as well as his baptism in the river Jordan by his cousin, John the Baptist. Stretching over three days, Timkat in Lalibela begins with the Tabots. These are replicas of the tablets containing God's commandments as handed down to Moses, subsequently placed in the Ark of Covenant. Each church has a Tabot, and those in the eleven subterranean churches are, at Timkat, removed with great ceremony from their altars. This is tantamount to a temporary decommissioning of the buildings as a place of worship since the Tabot in each is the most sacred object, just as the Ark itself was once the centrepiece of the Jewish Temple.

Such a major undertaking happens at Timkat so that the Tabots can be glimpsed by the faithful as they are carried, wrapped in colourful velvet cloths, on the head of a priest from each of the churches out through the tunnels and up the staircases that lead up to ground level. They spend their first night in a great tent, pitched nearby, where chanting and prayer goes on through the night. The tent is next to a large cross-shaped blue pool, which represents the river Jordan – like the drainage ditch in the pits. The next morning, vast crowds gather as the priests bless the water. Vibrant, elaborately fringed umbrellas are held up against the fierce sun (they are also said to signify the presence of the Holy Spirit) over the heads of the clerics as many present choose to renew their religious vows by, in imitation of Christ, immersing themselves in the water.

This is spectacle rather than solemn ritual, a joyous, exuberant occasion, somewhat similar to a summer afternoon in the country with youngsters jumping in, splashing, shouting and having a ball. Even the priests dance as they lead the chanting. The waters in the pool are also believed to have miraculous healing powers. Those with disabilities are present in large numbers while bathing in the waters for a childless woman is said to gain her God's help in conceiving.

The Tabots are then taken by a roundabout route back to their churches, accompanied by singing, drums, bells (*sitras*) and trumpets. Once safely returned, there is a communal feast, laid on by the people for their priests, and washed down by *tej*, the local delicacy, a honey and eucalyptus drink.

These rituals, like much else at Lalibela, are shaped not so much by an ecclesiastical rulebook, or by clerical dictate, but simply by the way they have always been done. That, therefore, is the way they will continue to be done. It is a pattern that allows the Orthodox faithful, when within its precincts, to turn their backs for a moment in time on the logic of the modern world that treats everything as provisional, capable of development and adaption in line with the latest trend or discovery. With that unbending attachment to the eternally unchanging, all the efforts of historians, archaeologists and the flock of experts who periodically descend on the eleven churches to find an explanation for why they are here, on this remote, rocky escarpment, are somehow irrelevant. They float over the heads of many of today's pilgrims, just as the outside world floats over the roofs of the subterranean pits where pilgrims gather. This is instead a world apart, a world moreover where a door is left open to the transcendent dimension missing elsewhere.

CHAPTER SIX

LOURDES, MEDJUGORJE AND THE MARIAN SHRINES
MARY AND THE MIRACLES

'All sites of pilgrimage have this in common: they are believed to be places where miracles once happened, and may happen again.'

Victor and Edith Turner, *Image and Pilgrimage in Christian Culture* (1978)[1]

In October 1987, Jean-Pierre Bely was persuaded by friends to go with them to the French Catholic shrine of Lourdes. A former intensive-care nurse, he had been suffering with reduced mobility for twelve years and had been forced to give up work when multiple sclerosis was finally diagnosed. At the time of his trip, the disease had taken over his body so much that the 51-year-old rarely got out of bed and couldn't walk a step. In the small town in the shadow of the Pyrenees, he had to be pushed in his wheelchair to the grotto, the exact spot where, in 1858, a peasant girl, Bernadette Soubirous, had described how the Virgin Mary had appeared to her eighteen times in the preceding weeks.

Bely was blessed by a priest in the grotto and recalled later how immediately he had the sense that the world began turning around him. Taken to a sickroom, he felt a deep cold in his bones. 'But slowly it got warmer and warmer until it felt like a fire burning through the whole of my body. I was overwhelmed by it. I heard this voice, like an order: "Get up and walk!" And then all of a sudden I found myself sitting up on the bed. I started to touch the back of my hands [and] realized that I had regained mobility and sensitivity in my spine and shoulders that had been blocked for years.'[2]

In the years immediately after Bernadette Soubirous shared details of the apparitions she had seen, pilgrims had flocked to Lourdes in great numbers. The local bishop had endorsed no fewer than seven miraculous cures from physical illnesses caused by the water from the spring that Jesus' mother had caused to start running. His actions alarmed the Vatican, however, which officially took charge of assessing all claims of miracles there. For the past 130 years, that work has been carried out on its behalf by the Lourdes Medical Bureau, which tests all such reports before a committee of medical experts. If they can find a scientific explanation, the case is rejected. If they cannot, after many subsequent rounds of scrutiny, it is officially approved. The Bureau says that it receives, on average, thirty-five accounts of miracle cures each year. Only sixty-seven in total have been officially authenticated by the Vatican. Formally approved in 1999, Bely's is the most recent. After being summoned that day in the sickroom to get up and walk, he did just that, and has been doing it ever since.

✻

The journey along pilgrimage trails often includes at least some sort of nod towards healing, whether the ambition be to walk into fitness, to step outside the humdrum tracks of everyday routine so as to tune in to a different, more purifying, inner rhythm, or to be liberated, as Bely was, from physical or mental illness. At Catholicism's Marian shrines, however, this broad and often unspoken hope has been distilled into a particularly potent, holy and enduring formula that draws pilgrims from all around the world. It has been Christianity that arguably most thoroughly integrated miraculous healing into its credo. In the four gospels' accounts of Jesus, he is seen regularly dispensing miraculous cures: from leprosy (the gospel of Matthew), making blind people see (Mark), telling those with paralysis to get up and walk (Luke), and, even, raising the dead Lazarus to life (John). The shrines on the Catholic pilgrim map build on such stories to claim that, through the intercession of his mother, Mary, similar results can still be achieved today.

This assertion flies, of course, in the face of reason in our secular times. Plenty of otherwise loyal mass-going Catholics also struggle with the idea that, in these specific locations, God is providing a tangible, physical form of proof of his existence that is so well-tailored to our human desires. Annually, an estimated thirty-five million people visit such shrines, at Guadalupe in Mexico, Fátima in Portugal, Medjugorje in former Yugoslavia, Knock in Ireland and a host of other smaller versions around the globe, some of which date back almost a thousand years. And they are just the latest manifestation of a yearning for divine healing that stretches back further still, as the British-born, Catholic-raised, Mexico-based surrealist painter Leonora Carrington suggested in her celebrated mural, *El Mundo Mágico de los Mayans*. In it, she depicts the Virgin of Guadalupe, carried aloft by worshippers, who have the faces of the animal spirits that were part of the worship of indigenous faiths in Mexico before the arrival of Catholicism.

The original Marian apparitions at Guadalupe took place in 1531. Almost half a millennium earlier, close to the east coast of England, at Walsingham in Norfolk, in 1061, Mary was reported to have appeared to a devout local noblewoman, Richeldis de Faverches, and commanded her to build a replica of the 'Holy House' of Nazareth, where the child Jesus had been raised. This apparition coincided with the rise of the cult of the Virgin Mary, both in Church teaching (it had not been prominent in the early centuries of Christianity and goes well beyond what is written of Mary in the gospels) and in the popular mind. In an organization dominated by men in its upper clerical reaches, the figure of Mary as intercessor in chief on behalf of humankind in heaven had broad appeal in congregations where women were in the majority but had no official role.

Lady Richeldis set about doing as Mary had instructed her. With its replica Holy House, its holy well where healing waters flowed, and its great abbey, Walsingham became one of the major Marian shrines of medieval Europe. It drew pilgrims who reached it by a network of routes lined by chapels, abbeys and other places offering hospitality to travellers that spread out from the shrine to Norwich, Ely, London and, even, via a treacherous path over the mud flats of the tidal basin of the Wash, to the north and west of England and beyond. About 2 kilometres outside the shrine, at the Slipper Chapel, pilgrims would remove their shoes and, as an extra act of penance, complete the last leg barefoot. (Such bodily abnegation was – and remains – something of a pilgrim staple. On the last Sunday in July devout Irish Catholics at Croagh Patrick in County Mayo, where the saint fasted for forty days in the fifth century, still climb the stony mountain without shoes.)

Every English king from Edward I to Henry VIII made a pilgrimage to Walsingham, the latter in 1511 to give thanks to Mary for her intercession with God over granting a much-wanted son, Prince Henry, to him and his wife, Catherine of Aragon. But the child died within two months of his birth, and the same king was later to sever ties with the papacy over his wish to divorce and remarry in his search for a male heir. In the resulting breach with Rome, Henry ordered the dissolution of the monasteries in 1536 and the abbey that was at the centre of the life of Walsingham was left in ruins.

The site reverted to being a small country village again. Yet the legacy of what had once been there was never quite forgotten in the 350 years that it slumbered out of sight. At the end of the nineteenth century a revival began, what buildings were left were restored, and where they had disappeared replicas were erected. Today, it once again welcomes 100,000 pilgrims each year, though the healing of the wounds of the English Reformation does not yet stretch to combining into one the separate Catholic and Anglican shrines that now exist there, alongside a small Orthodox chapel.

Walsingham's revival means that England is once again among the sixty-four countries around the world where the Catholic Church has a national Marian shrine, approved by its bishops. Only ten such places globally, however, carry the Vatican's gold-standard imprimatur as having been definitively accepted as having witnessed apparitions of Mary, and their (in Catholicism) natural corollary, miracle cures.

Yet miracles come in all shapes and sizes. The vast majority of modern-day visitors come looking for that otherworldly spiritual succour that exists in the spirit of such pilgrim places, but some continue to seek a physical cure. And so time spent in them involves the larger band of more modest seekers witnessing the faith of the small number of visibly sick and ailing who come to embrace the literal truth of reports of Mary's special blessing on the place. Often the latter have endured uncomfortable journeys, stretching fragile or failing bodies to the limit. Their pilgrimage has little in common with the athleticism of the Camino trek. It is one invested with a more urgent sort of hope for restoration of health. 'The sick don't just count, here,' one wheelchair-user wrote home during a visit to Lourdes, 'they come first'. That is certainly the case in a practical way in the queue for the shrine's baths, where visitors are briefly, tenderly but efficiently immersed in water from the spring that Mary is believed to have created. It is true, too, in a spiritual sense. For the fit and healthy who are also drawn there, all empirical, worldly questions and doubts about miracles, that tendency to regard the gospel talk of Jesus' miracles as more metaphor than fact, is often put aside. There is a curious but powerful knock-on effect of being alongside and among so many who believe absolutely in the power of Marian shrines to transform the daily realities of their lives. Their act of faith, so tangible and potent, gives Lourdes – and the other Marian shrines like it – a special aura, a sign of contradiction to the world beyond their walls and sanctuaries.

In recent times, though, the Catholic authorities have gently downplayed that very real expectation of miraculous cures at the pilgrim shrines it runs or endorses. The row after row of discarded crutches that used to hang from the roof of the grotto at Lourdes, like the serried ranks of foot soldiers of the Lord marching to a heavenly beat, have been quietly removed and locked away.

It was part of a more general waning in official championing of Marian pilgrimages in the years after Catholicism's reforming and modernizing Second Vatican Council of the mid-1960s. The advent, however, of the Polish pope, John Paul II, in 1978 reversed this trend. 'Before him,' says the Catholic-educated cultural historian and author of the acclaimed *Alone of All Her Sex: The Myth and Cult of the Virgin Mary*, Marina Warner, 'the papacy had developed an austere anxiety about too much Marian enthusiasm, too much popular piety, and all the pageant that went with it, but he let it rip. He did more than any pope in modern times to revive her cult. Numbers of those going on pilgrimage rose. We saw the triumph of the sensuous side of Catholicism.'[3]

John Paul was certainly an enthusiast for visiting Marian pilgrimage sites, including going three times to Fátima during his pontificate and twice to Lourdes, the second time in 2004, a year before his death, when he was visibly ailing and struggling to speak. To the 200,000-strong crowd who gathered to greet him, he was sharing in their yearning that, when everything else in twenty-first-century knowledge and expertise has failed to address their afflictions, divine intervention, via Mary, would come to the rescue – if not to effect a cure, then to ease the pain and smooth the way for what was to come after death. Whatever the Church's current caution around Marian pilgrimage shrines, then, that balm remains unmistakably on offer in the Lourdes sanctuary, in the shadow of the white, neo-Gothic Basilica of the Immaculate Conception, during the daily afternoon procession behind an elaborate holder containing the blessed sacrament (the disc of unleavened bread used at holy communion, believed by Catholics to be the body of Christ), and each evening, as pilgrims carrying candles circle around, reciting the rosary, the sequence of prayers associated with Mary. 'I was aware', wrote the award-winning Irish novelist Colm Tóibín, brought up Catholic, of his visit to Lourdes as a young man drifting away from the Church, 'of having entered another atmosphere'.[4]

Evidence of how widespread are its reputation and renown can be discerned in the fact that only Paris, in the whole of France, has more hotel beds than Lourdes (and this despite four of the other ten Vatican-approved shrines also being in France). This also perhaps gives a clue that Lourdes is no longer the exclusively or 'hard-core' Catholic place of previous decades. The precipitous decline in church-going and church-membership figures seen of late in France, as in every Western country, have had an impact. There was a marked fall in numbers of visitors at Lourdes in the early noughties, by up to a quarter in group pilgrimages, resulting in a corresponding financial deficit in the accounts of the church body that runs the shrine. It prompted a rethink on how to promote Lourdes and widen its appeal by replacing lost believers in its pilgrim ranks with the more generally spiritually curious who might have already tried out the Camino trail. Indeed, the classic *Camino Frances* route begins not so far away from Lourdes at Saint-Jean-Pied-de-Port, at the eastern foot of the Pyrenees near the border of France and Spain. You can now have two experiences for the price of one, flying into Lourdes (which has its own airport) and then setting out from there to reach one of the traditional Camino starting points.

❁

In the millennium-long history of Marian shrines, Medjugorje is a novice. On an early midsummer evening, 24 June 1981, a group of local youngsters, some of whom lived in this deeply Catholic area of rural Hercegovina in what was then Yugoslavia, others with family connections there and visiting for the summer holidays, described jointly seeing a strange light on the lower slopes of the local hill known as Podbrdo (now 'Apparition Hill'). Within it was a beautiful, young Mary, holding the infant Jesus. The sightings continued daily until 1 July, always at the same time and in the same place.

Within five days news of what was going on had spread to such an extent that 15,000 pilgrims turned up from all around the area to watch as the six visionaries, aged between 10 to 17, stood or knelt, looking awe-struck, their eyes fixed beatifically on a spot in front of them, their lips moving silently. Afterwards, they explained to the crowds that they had been listening to, and questioning, the 'Gospa' – the Croatian word for the Virgin Mary (though located in Bosnia-Hercegovina since the break-up of Yugoslavia, the six hamlets that make up Medjugorje are religiously and ethnically an extension of nearby predominantly Catholic Croatia).

There is much in Medjugorje's story (its name means 'between the mountains') that chimes with what has gone on elsewhere in Catholicism over the centuries. Mixed in, too, are intriguing details that do not, and which suggest that, even in the still largely Catholic world of destinations bound up with Mary and miracles, changes are afoot that reflect an opening up of this once introspective part of the pilgrim world.

To start with what is familiar. The youth – and devotees would say the innocence – of the Mejudgorje seers is striking. They were mostly teenagers – like Bernadette Soubirous, or Benoîte Rencur-rel, the 16-year-old shepherdess who told of seeing Mary in May 1664 at Laus in the French Alps, or 14-year-old Mélanie Calvat, who along with 11-year-old Maximim Giraud, reported being visited by a weeping Mary in September 1846 in the farming community of La Salette, just over 48 kilometres away from Laus. Both of these last two apparitions in southeast France are, with Lourdes, on the Vatican's approved list.

Then there is the interchangeable backdrop of where these apparitions occur. All happen in impoverished rural areas steeped in Catholicism. Medjugorje, in June 1981, was every bit as remote as Lourdes in 1858 or Walsingham in 1061. It was a backwater where corn, tobacco and vines grew in the fertile red soil of a valley that stood in the shadow of high, barren mountains.

The content of the messages, too, has substantial overlap with other such reports, above all in stressing the need to retain or return to the traditional practices of the faith, such as prayer, fasting, reading the scriptures, going to the sacraments, and saying the Rosary. This has made some sceptical. The late twentieth-century wandering pilgrim and writer, the Jesuit Gerard Hughes, whose bestselling accounts of walks to Rome and Jerusalem have been mentioned earlier, publicly voiced his doubts about what he dubbed 'apparition piety', suggesting it had a 'special appeal to people of rigid views, usually those on the far right politically and theologically, because such a spirituality does not challenge their thinking'.[5] For him, pilgrimage should be about testing existing beliefs not confirming them.

And a final point of conformity: as at La Salette in 1846, and later with Lucia dos Santos and her cousins Francisco and Jacinta Marto, the three very young seers at rural Fátima in Portugal in 1917, the Virgin Mary at Medjugorje entrusted the visionaries with grave secrets, instructing them that they were only to be revealed at a later, prescribed date. The parallels between Medjugorje and Fátima are especially striking. In both places, the visionaries claim to have seen the sun spin in the sky, as did pilgrims who travelled there to watch them at the time of their apparitions.

'I could look right into the sun, which appeared to be a flat disc, off-white in colour, spinning rapidly,' the Jesuit academic Father Robert Faricy, of Rome's Pontifical Gregorian University, recalled of his visit in the 1980s to Medjugorje. 'From time to time light pulsed out from behind the disc. I tried to see if my blinking coincided with these pulsations of fire, but it was not so. I found that I could look away without my eyes being dazzled. Afterwards the sun returned to its normal brilliance, and for the next hour, before it set, I could no longer look at it directly.'[6]

Like other miracle shrines, the small village of Medjugorje expanded quickly, and messily, to accommodate, feed and sustain, spiritually and physically, the sudden influx of pilgrims. In its case, however, it faced particular obstacles from the then Yugoslavian authorities, hostile to organized religion, and suspicious that what was happening there was a political attempt to give a Catholic charge to Croatian nationalism at a time when the Serb-dominated federal structure of Yugoslavia was coming apart at the seams. They therefore tried (unsuccessfully) to close off the village to pilgrims, then detained and jailed the parish priest, and even carted the six visionaries off to doctors and psychiatrists in a fruitless search of proof that they were being manipulated or were delusional.

The history of religion, when it clashes with controlling political systems, demonstrates time and time again that efforts to suppress it may work in the short term, but ultimately can only make it grow stronger. That was especially true at Medjugorje in its early days and remains part of the spirit of the place. Within six months of the first reports, despite the efforts of the authorities, 100,000 pilgrims had come, many of them walking from all parts of Croatia and beyond. Total numbers over four decades now stand at more than forty million.

Among those drawn to the site, there have, once again, been people searching for spiritual healing. 'My whole attitude to life had altered,' wrote the Catholic historian Desmond Seward in his 1993 account of a pilgrimage to Medjugorje, of waking up there on the first full day of his pilgrimage. 'All depression, all worries had gone. I felt greater peace of mind than I could ever remember.'[7] And there are those, too, seeking a physical cure. Though it has no spring of healing water like Lourdes, thousands of miracles have been reported at Medjugorje. In September 2003, Colleen Willard, a 52-year-old devoutly Catholic schoolteacher from Chicago, arrived with her husband, John. She was so ill – with an inoperable brain tumour and various other diagnosed conditions which had left her in constant pain and unable to walk – that airlines refused to accept her booking. The pull of the place was too strong, however, so she persevered and persuaded them. Once there, Willard first met one of the six visionaries, Vicka Ivankovic (several still live in and around Medjugorje, while others have moved further afield), who prayed over her.

Next the mother-of-three attended mass in the modern parish church of Saint James, whose twin towers dominate the shrine's landscape. As she received the consecrated bread at holy communion, Willard later recalled, she felt a powerful sensation of heat leaving her body, and with it the pain that had crippled her. She was able to get up out of her wheelchair and walk out of the church. Some fifteen years on, she remains untroubled by pain.

There are aspects, though, of Medjugorje that are all of its own and shine a light on a distinctly contemporary pilgrimage phenomenon. In all other reports of Marian apparitions, they have been short-lived, some just a single day, as at Knock in western Ireland in 1879, or at most up to four months at Laus in the seventeenth century. To this day, though, the six seers of Medjugorje continue to report receiving messages from Mary; some come occasionally, others weekly, monthly or annually. They are faithfully relayed to devotees via social media. Medjugorje is the first pilgrimage shrine of the Internet age and has successfully fed online that spiritual hunger without the requirement to travel to a particular place. A daily flow of messages animates and gives hope to a vast like-minded, receptive e-community around the globe.

After a period of initial scepticism over events at Medjugorje, encouraged by the hostility of the local Bishop of Mostar who declared them as 'the fruit of fraud, disobedience to the Church and disease', the Vatican has been looking on more favourably of late. There were some official efforts by Rome, in the early days, to discourage pilgrims from even going, but in such matters even the most loyal Catholic pilgrim has long followed their heart rather than the rules laid down by their priests and bishops, operating on the basis that there is no harm in taking a look. And there is, arguably, even a certain pull around being a pioneer that still makes Medjugorje enthusiasts keen, if given the chance, to talk it up as if revealing a secret.

In its ongoing examination of events at Medjugorje, the Vatican has carefully grouped the reports of apparitions into two categories: those that took place within a short period at the end of June 1981, and all those that have come since. In other words, they have drawn a line between those that fit the traditional pattern, and those that suggest apparitions go on and on. Towards the first, the report of a church commission in the spring of 2017 was generally positive, though not to the extent that it was ready formally to authorize them as authentic. Pope Francis has since appointed his own personal representative to the shrine, and speaks of it approvingly in public, laying special emphasis on what he refers to as the difference between 'the spiritual fact' and 'the pastoral fact'. For him the important thing is the pastoral fact, 'that people go there and convert'.

His words bring us up against that aspect of pilgrimage that is about evangelization. All Christians, of course, were told by Jesus to go and spread the 'Good News' to others, and if his immediate circle of apostles hadn't been so diligent in doing as they were told after his crucifixion then there might not have been a Christian church at all. In the modern age, however, zeal in evangelization is something many mainstream believers shun, and is noticeably absent at other pilgrim trails and sites.

In Medjugorje, whether by divine intention, human design, or simply the power of a place that is so wrapped up in a distinctly and robustly traditional Catholic view of faith, conversions are very much still in vogue. It harks back to another and older way of looking at pilgrimage: as a journey into making a formal religious commitment to an institution. As Pope Francis's words highlight, Medjugorje has gained a reputation for convincing those non-Catholics who go there not just to deepen their spiritual life but also to join the Church.

Alongside this, though, Medjugorje is also markedly more ecumenical than many other Marian shrines. Welcoming other faiths and inspiring their members to convert would, at first glance, seem to sit uneasily together. Yet, from earliest days, Medjugorje has attracted substantial numbers of both Orthodox Christians, often from Serbian backgrounds in the ethnic mix of what was then Yugoslavia, as well as Muslims, especially from the nearby town of Mostar, where they represent around half of the population. One of the very first reports of a miracle cure at Medjugorje concerned a young, sickly Orthodox girl, after her family had taken her to Apparition Hill.

This multi-faith dimension, though unusual at Marian shrines, should in many ways be no surprise. The Qur'an gives special importance to Maryam, or Mary, where she is the only woman named in its pages, while among the Orthodox – separated from Western Christianity since the eleventh century – there is a deep devotion to the 'Aeiparthenos', 'the Ever Virgin Mary', who is also known by the title 'Theotokos' or 'god-bearer/mother of God'. For Orthodox Christians, ancient and treasured icons of Mary and her child have long been the subject of great veneration. Even today Orthodox pilgrims will travel many kilometres to be in the presence of such icons, taking home copies to put on public display in their own towns and villages.

At Medjugorje, this ability to bring together people of different, often antagonistic, faith traditions runs much deeper, into the soil itself. These remote villages sit within a region that has experienced bitter bloody ethnic and religious tensions, not just in the Balkan Wars of the 1990s that broke up Yugoslavia, and in the fragile peace that has existed since, but also as part of the centuries-old historical disputes between people of different beliefs, with Catholics, Orthodox and Muslim all laying claim to these lands.

Christianity was established in the area where Medjugorje sits around the seventh century. When, 400 years later, the western and eastern halves of the Church split, locals remained loyal to Rome, though Constantinople/Istanbul, centre of the Orthodox world, was geographically closer. Being on the frontline of denominational boundaries gave the local Catholics, all Croats, a certain pride and resilience, which then sustained them, with the unflinching support of Franciscan priests, through the four centuries of not always benign rule by the Muslim rulers of the Ottoman Empire. Only in 1878, when these overlords were driven back by the Catholic Habsburgs, sweeping down from Austria, did the region around Medjugorge finally experience alignment between its political rulers in the Austro-Hungarian Empire and its Catholic faith.

The local Franciscan parish was founded in 1892 but, in the Serbian-dominated kingdom of Yugoslavia that existed between the First and Second World Wars, Croats still felt themselves, and their religion, to be oppressed by the Serbian Orthodox Church. As a defiant response, in 1933 on Krizevac ('Mount of the Cross'), the 520-metre high peak that overlooks Medjugorje, a giant cross was erected to mark the 1,900th anniversary of Jesus' death and resurrection (said, by the Church, to have taken place in 33 AD). It was intended as a means of invoking his on-going protection against hostile neighbours as well as against the fierce weather that too often ruined their crops.

When the Second World War engulfed Yugoslavia, age-old ethnic and religious tensions resurfaced. In Croatia, some, but by no means all, Catholic Croats collaborated in 1941 with the invading Germans, establishing a compliant puppet government under the leader of the Ustase movement, Ante Pavelić, an extremist who was fiercely hostile to the Serbs and their Orthodox religion. Both sides suffered and both sides carried out massacres. One took place within the parish boundaries of Medjugorje, at the station in the hamlet of Surmanci. On 6 August 1941, 600 Serbian Orthodox Christians from Prebilovci, mothers, infants and girls under 10, were unloaded from a train by the Ustase, with two Catholic priests standing watching, then marched into the mountains and thrown down from a precipice into a pit. Those who were not killed by the fall were left to die of their injuries. Elsewhere tales of forced conversions by the Ustase of Orthodox Christians to Catholicism in nearby villages were legion, while, in February 1945, 30 kilometres away from Medjugorje, at the Franciscan monastery of Siroki Brijeg, thirty Catholic friars were slaughtered by Partisans, mainly Serbian troops loyal to Marshal Tito, who believed Ustase fighters were being given shelter there.

At the end of the war, Yugoslavia became a communist, authoritarian federal state under Tito, keen always to subdue those old religious and ethnic tensions. So, in the early days of the apparitions at Medjugorje, the authorities could only see the risk of the reports causing a flare-up. Yet such an approach ignored the content of the messages conveyed by the visionaries. Mary was repeatedly urging peace and a healing of old wounds. Medjugorje was, it seemed, intended as a place of atonement for past atrocities and hatreds, not as a battlefield in a religious war. Nonetheless, almost ten years to the day from Mary's first reported appearance, a war began as Yugoslavia fell apart following Tito's death. As the most powerful player in the old federal regime, Serbia resisted and, by ethnic cleansing, sought to carve out a greater Serbia from hitherto mixed areas beyond its boundaries.

The frontline of the conflict came within a few kilometres of Medugorje, with many of its resident population of 2,000 fleeing as refugees to Croatia. Mostar was occupied by the Serbs and its world-renowned Ottoman bridge over the river Neretva destroyed. There were Serb military positions beyond Apparition Hill in April 1992 and those who had remained in Medjugorje, including two of the visionaries, were forced to hide in bomb shelters until the siege was lifted in June.

The shrine – some said miraculously – survived largely undamaged, a couple of cluster bombs having done little harm. There were even stories of two Serbian pilots in Russian MiG fighters who defied orders and refused to drop their bombs on Saint James's church. Medjugorje emerged from the war with its reputation as a haven of peace enhanced, and it started welcoming pilgrims again in the summer of 1992, though the local airport at Mostar did not reopen until 1998. What had happened gave urgency to Mary's words, passed on by the seers, of the need to seek peace and reconciliation.

One local Franciscan priest, Father Svetozar Kraljevic, has gone so far as to write that 'the blood of the martyrs of the Church' over the centuries – he mentions in particular the thirty Franciscans murdered in 1945 at nearby Siroki Brijeg – 'brought Our Lady to

Medjugorje'.[8] In other words, it is not just the landscape of natural beauty and great and enduring faith that draws pilgrims to this spot, but also the riposte that it offers to all the brutality, butchery and spilt blood that has marked out its history.

CHAPTER SEVEN

THE NORTH WALES PILGRIM'S WAY
CELTIC REVIVAL

※

'There is an island there is no going
to but in a small boat the way
the saints went, travelling the gallery
of the frightened faces of
the long-drowned, munching the gravel
of its beaches'

R. S. THOMAS, 'PILGRIMAGES' (1978)[1]

Celtic monks were great wanderers, by land and sea, both as Christian missionaries and as seekers after a purer relationship with God that they believed was to be found by immersing themselves in the natural world. Often quite literally. The sixth-century Irish saint Brendan the Voyager, according to a celebrated account of his life,[2] sailed west down the river Shannon and into the Atlantic Ocean in the company of some of his brethren, heading out to a beautiful 'Land of Promise'. Some academics take this literally and speculate that his destination was the Canary Islands, others that the 'great crystal pillars' referred to in the text as part of hell were either icebergs or Iceland. Celtic mythology, though, is vague, opaque and possessed of many layers of meaning. It laid a heavy emphasis on the metaphysical not the physical, symbolism not solidity. Heading ever west into the setting sun was, in the words of Brendan's Voyage, to 'wonder at the glory of God's creation'. A key concept for the Celts was the notion of finding God 'in exile' – the belief that, if they travelled to the furthest reaches of the known world, they would be closer to heaven. It was thus both a spiritual and a physical endeavour.

Because of their isolation, islands held a particular fascination for the Celtic Christians of the first millennium CE, either as a stepping stone to paradise or as a proxy for it. Bardsey, one end of the ancient North Wales Pilgrim's Way that has been revived in the early years of the twenty-first century by a group inspired by the Camino, was one such place. It enjoyed a reputation far and wide for floating somewhere between earth and heaven. Ynys Enlli, to give its Welsh name, is shaped like a whale basking on the surface of the Irish Sea, nuzzling the end of the Llyn (pronounced Clean) Peninsula along which today's 225-kilometre pilgrim path passes. If the hump of the whale's upper quarters is the modest hill (in Welsh it becomes a mountain – Mynydd Enlli) that faces out from Bardsey across the nearly 5-kilometre sound to the mainland, its long tapering tail is the westward-extending stretch of low-lying farmland that looks out onto apparently endless sea. The Celtic pilgrims who gathered on the whale's hindmost part 1,500 years ago were convinced that, once in this spot where the gap between heaven and earth was shorter than at any other point, they might breathe in on the breeze something of the unknown spiritual domain that lay just beyond the horizon.

The term 'Celtic Christianity' is treated with caution by historians, implying as it does an organized grouping or movement that was at odds with the centralizing, rules-based tentacles that were spreading out from the Church of Rome in the centuries after Jesus' death. In reality, though, there was something much more piecemeal: groups, often led by holy men, who typically gathered on the fringes of the land, where they practised a version of Christianity that accepted many of the doctrines promoted by Rome but also, in their fierce independence, developed their own particular way of doing things, often drawing for inspiration on existing pagan wisdom in order to fashion something we now call Celtic.[3]

In 516, it was precisely such a group of determined individuals who arrived on the shores of Bardsey, with the warrior monk Cadfan at its head. He was a Breton nobleman, inspired by God, who had travelled from France to the west coast of Wales, along with some of his pious highborn friends. All were steeped in the scholarly, itinerant, earthy, mystical Celtic tradition, which was proving so powerful in shaping the early centuries of Christianity. They established a string of abbeys, culminating in the far-flung Bardsey. Their direct inspiration was the Desert Fathers, hermits and ascetics such as Saint Antony (c. 251–356) who had dedicated their lives to prayer and hard manual labour in loosely knit communities in the wilderness of the Egyptian desert. In imitation, these Celtic monks sought out wild places where they would have no distractions from being with God. Cadfan referred to Bardsey – where the ruins of his abbey remain a focus for pilgrim visitors – as his 'resurrection'.

Part of this linked chain of Welsh coastal monasteries and abbeys was the one at Saint David's, at the southern end of the sweeping curve of Cardigan Bay. The 'Rule' that shaped life at the monastery – drawn up by David, the founder, reputedly the grandson of Ceredig ap Cunedda, king of Ceredigion, and later patron saint of Wales – gives an insight into what life on Bardsey would have been like in the sixth century. The community was at one with nature – and hence God. No animals were to be used to plough the land. That was to be done by the monks themselves. They drank only water, ate only bread with salt and herbs, and avoided all meat and alcohol. Outside of work, time was spent in prayer, reading and writing. No personal possessions were allowed.

Such a pared-down approach to life had a strong resonance in the final decades of the twentieth century as part of a widespread Celtic revival that, in the late 1990s, saw *Anam Cara*, a collection of ancient Celtic wisdom put together by the Irish poet and former Catholic priest John O'Donohue, become an international word-of-mouth bestseller.[4] And that appeal has continued and even grown in the twenty-first century. Those who walk in the shadow of those early monks on the North Wales Pilgrim's Way can cast a longing look back at a sustainable, spiritual example that may feed into the sense in them that something has been lost in modern religious experience as in modern life itself, especially in an age overshadowed by environmental degradation and the threat of climate change.

The blurred boundaries between fact and fable that character-izes the Celtic approach are accommodating of all shades of opinion, while the landmarks of the North Wales Pilgrim's Way, some of which have their origins in the seventh century, offer a ready opportunity to embrace an earlier age, whether it be at the start, with the remains of the medieval Basingwerk Abbey in northeast Wales, once a pilgrims' hostel serving the ancient healing shrine at Holywell, or Bardsey itself at the western end of the route.

The Synod of Whitby in 664 marked the beginning of Rome's efforts to wind in the independence of the Celtic thread of Christi-anity in Britain. It took place in the northeast of England, another region with a strong Celtic influence that radiated out of the not-quite-so-inaccessible Holy Island of Lindisfarne, reached from the mainland over mud flats only at low tide. In the wake of the meeting at Whitby, centralized authority was increasingly felt in the form of standardized rituals, overseen by a system of dioceses and bishops answerable to the Pope. Yet the very isolation that had first drawn Cadfan to Bardsey enabled it to maintain much of its freedom, as reported as late as the twelfth century by the traveller and chronicler Gerald of Wales, who described it as, 'inhabited by very religious monks'. He added, in a line still quoted, that the island 'has this wonderful peculiarity that the oldest people die first, because diseases are uncommon, and scarcely any die except from extreme old age'.[5]

The *Book of Llandaff*, compiled in the middle of the twelfth century, mentions the same aura of holiness on Bardsey, yet puts it down not to the age of the monks who lived there, but rather to the – potentially related – fact that 'the bodies of 20,000 holy confessors and martyrs' were buried there. This was still a windswept anteroom to heaven on the very edge of the known world, both holy *and* healthy, because it stood apart from the world.

And, it should be added, holy, healthy *and* blessed. Legend has it that it was an angel who promised Saint Lleuddad, Cadfan's successor as abbot, when on his death bed, that henceforth no one on the island would die while there was someone older living there. As with Celtic Christianity in general, Bardsey in particular was awash with legends that spoke to a higher truth. Their survival is an indication of its importance as a place of pilgrimage in the Middle Ages. Miraculous stories are not repeated about somewhere no one has heard of or visited. One has it that Saint Llawddog, a sixth-century descendant of royal blood from the north of Britain, once milked a cow over a well on Bardsey and afterwards the well produced milk instead of water to nourish visitors. Another suggests that Bardsey is the final resting place of that central figure in Arthurian legend, and Britain's sacred landscape, Merlin the magician.

By the thirteenth century, however, the abbey seems finally to have relinquished its traditional independence when it became a branch of the Augustinian order, established to buttress the authority of the Pope in Rome. At various stages thereafter it is recorded as holding land on the mainland and receiving tithes from Aberdaron, the fishing village at the tip of the Llyn Peninsula, but it was in decline. By 1537, when it was dissolved, along with all monasteries on the orders of Henry VIII after his break with Rome, Bardsey Abbey contributed the meagre sum of £46 to the king's commissioners.

The accuracy of that 20,000 figure – and therefore of its wider importance as a place of pilgrimage – has been questioned by recent generations of historians. If it is true, they point out, it would mean that there are roughly forty-four corpses under each of Bardsey's 450 acres. One suggestion is that at least some of the 20,000 saints were the survivors of a royal massacre in 613 of the monks of Bangor, another Celtic monastery founded by Deniol, a holy hermit who went on to be Bishop of Bangor. They fled for their lives to Bardsey, in the hope that putting water between them and their pursuers might save their lives. The escaped monks ended up seeing out their days on the island, in a kind of glorious haven for outlaws.

According to another theory, many of the 20,000 did not come here as pilgrims in their lifetime and then stayed on to die, but rather arrived after death to be buried in what was regarded by Welsh Christians in the area as the ultimate holy soil. In the twelfth century, in the summer months when the tides were generally more benign, boats would pass up the great sweep of Cardigan Bay from the south, collecting the corpses of wealthy, recently dead Christians from tiny stone churches built on or next to the beaches, and then transporting them to Bardsey for burial. To secure such a resting place, in the company of saints and closer to heaven than most, the deceased or their families would have had to bequeath part of their wealth to the upkeep of the abbey on Bardsey.

The 20,000 were not saints in the official sense. Typically, Celtic Christians had a distinctive notion of what it was to be a saint. Their belief was far removed from what is promoted today, principally by Catholicism. It makes such decisions centrally, and awards the title only to those who have been judged by its bureaucracy, in a process that takes decades if not centuries, to possess a set list of exceptional qualities in life, plus the ability to intercede from beyond the grave to make miracles possible for those who pray to them. By contrast, in Celtic circles being labelled a saint often indicated simply that the person in question was a Christian leader, a missionary, a hermit, or even 'just' a good Christian.

In such a context the claim that 20,000 devout souls may have been buried on Bardsey in the centuries following Cadfan's arrival is not so implausible. Moreover, it makes the whole place more attractive to the estimated 10,000 people who today walk the North Wales Pilgrim's Way to reconnect with Celtic values. This isn't the graveyard of the pious heroes of the Church, those who were a cut above the rest of humanity even in life, but rather the final home of those, like the pilgrims whatever their beliefs or none, who simply try to lead decent lives.

What also contributed to Bardsey's reputation for holiness – in the past and now – is that the crossing from the mainland involved, like Saint Brendan's voyage into the Atlantic, a strong and always present element of mortal danger. Pilgrimage to Bardsey is not just about making yourself spiritually open, or putting yourself in a place where (unlike in the rest of largely secular society) God's presence is mentioned regularly and openly. It is also about risking something physically, entrusting yourself to divine mercy. The sound between Bardsey and Aberdaron is reputedly the most treacherous stretch of water anywhere in the British Isles. It is better captured by Bardsey's Welsh name, Ynys Enlli, which translates as 'isle of the currents' or 'tide-race island'. Pilgrims who cross can expect to be thrown around a little as great surges of water funnel through the narrow strait. Wrecks were at one time big business on Bardsey. There used to be as many pirates there as saints, some said.

Present-day pilgrims are transported on a sturdy modern launch, capable of riding the waves. In medieval times they most likely would cross in a coracle, made of stretched leather on a light wooden frame, with no map and only oars and a finger in the wind to judge the weather conditions. Though it was less than 5 kilometres, it was considered so dangerous that the Pope himself reputedly declared that three pilgrimages to Bardsey were the equivalent of one to Rome. Inaccessibility and holiness were connected, as of course they are, according to Christian teaching, when it comes to heaven.

❋

May the road rise up to meet you.
May the wind be always at your back.
May the sun shine warm on your face,
the rains fall soft upon your fields
and until we meet again,
may God hold you in the palm of His hand.

This traditional Celtic blessing has been adopted by the North Wales Pilgrim's Way. It sums up both the spirit in which walkers take up the challenge it offers, and the ever-present connection to an earlier age that the route provides to all-comers. In early Christianity, the wind at your back would have been readily understood as the Holy Spirit, but for the new generation of pilgrims there is no requirement to talk of the visible in terms of the invisible. What is openly expressed, though, is the ambition that this trail should be regarded as the 'Welsh Camino'. In 2009, Jenny and Chris Potter had walked the Camino in Spain. On their return to North Wales – where Chris served as an archdeacon in Saint Asaph, which boasts the smallest Anglican cathedral in Britain, built on the site where another Celtic saint, Kentigern, established himself as a bishop in the sixth century – they were inspired to explore the history of the neglected pilgrim path that passed right by their doorstep.

It has been thanks to their efforts – a perfect illustration of the 'Camino effect' rippling outwards – that a route was identified, mapped, tested out in 2011, waymarked, and then officially opened in 2014, complete with its very own pilgrim's passport, which can be stamped at churches, shops and pubs on the way. In some places the trail mirrors the one original Celtic pilgrims would have taken, its identifying landmarks being small, low-lying ancient churches and sacred wells that are scattered all over the North Wales countryside, along with distinctive Celtic crosses such as the tall, thin tenth-century 'wheel cross' in a field at Maen Achwyfan in Flintshire on the route near the village of Llanasa ('the enclosure of Saint Asaph'). It features intricate knot patterns in its weather-beaten carvings, as well as a shadowy figure on the lower panel. Their exact meaning is lost in the mists of time – like a lot of things with Celtic Christianity. Meanwhile, one suggestion for this 'wheel cross' being in such a lonely location is that it marks what was once a hermit monk's cell, built to be far away from any distraction save nature and God.

Place names that begin with Llan- generally indicate a sacred past, but there are so many of them in North Wales it didn't really help in pinning down a definitive pilgrims' route. So, notably at Abergwyngregyn around the halfway point, where the route joins the already established Wales Coast Path, the Pilgrim's Way opts to make use of existing infrastructure. If this is not a perfect recreation, then it does successfully link four key locations from 1,300 years ago: Holywell, Gwytherin, Clynnog Fawr and Bardsey. The first three share a close association with two presiding presences on the pilgrimage, uncle and niece Saints Beuno and Winefride.

Like so many other Celtic monks Beuno, who died around 640, came from a privileged background. He embodied the missionary spirit that was a key part of vocation. His personal pilgrimage was as much about finding souls to convert as it was seeking personal enlightenment. After ordination in Bangor, now a popular starting point halfway along the Pilgrim's Way for those on a tight time schedule, he spent his days travelling all around North Wales, bringing people to a God whom he saw in every bit of the dramatic natural environment around him, bounded as it is by the sea on one side and the spectacular mountain range that includes Snowdon, Wales's highest peak, to the other. Often when he moved on after such a mission, he would leave behind a simple church building and a well. Water had special significance to Celtic Christians, who used 'triple immersion' in baptism ceremonies (in contrast to today when a tiny scoop of water is deemed sufficient). And Beuno was never happier, legend recounts, than when praying half-immersed in cold water, punishing his body to bring his soul closer to God.

Water also possessed healing powers, he believed. The pagan roots of this typically Celtic belief are plain. Indeed, one of the features of the North Wales Pilgrim's Way is that it encompasses, alongside Christian churches and crosses, pagan holy sites such as the stone circle at Penmaenmawr, and the 4,000-year-old yew in the churchyard at Llangernyw. On account of their extraordinary longevity – making them a symbol of (near) eternal life – yews held a special place in pre-Christian belief systems. Springs and wells, too, as well as groves of trees, were believed to be sacred, and became the backdrop to pagan rituals. Emerging Christianity sought not to confront and wipe away such patterns of worship, but rather to merge them in its own approach to the divine. Some anthropologists refer to this process of assimilation as 'baptizing the customs'.[6]

Legend has it that when he landed in Kent in 597, sent by Pope Gregory the Great to convert the English, the monk Augustine, the first Archbishop of Canterbury, conducted a ceremony in which he showered a yew with holy water in order to 'bring over' the whole species to Rome. The same thing happened throughout the country at pagan shrines to water deities. They became holy wells, whose waters could miraculously cure illnesses not through the intercession of nature deities, but rather of the one God whose son Jesus had saved humankind by his death and resurrection.

As with the later Marian shrines, these sacred sites combined pilgrimage with healing, but the source of their supernatural potential was not Christ's mother – her cult was a minor aspect of early Christianity – but rather God acting through chosen intermediaries such as Beuno. Most enduringly, this intervention happened at Holywell, the first major point that the pilgrim – *pererin* in Welsh – reaches on the route. Here Beuno's niece, Winifrede, a pious young noble woman, was rudely propositioned and then attacked by a local princeling. When she refused his advances and fought back, he drew his sword and cut off her head. Beuno, according to what became a popular medieval legend, happened to be preaching nearby in a church, and so came rushing to her aid, restoring her severed head to her body and bringing her back to life, 'only showing a slender scar running round the neck'. Where the head had touched the ground, it was told, a spring had miraculously appeared. At Winifrede's Well, that spring provides the ice-cold water in which pilgrims have been bathing for 1,300 years in the small town of Holywell. The shrine even managed to survive intact during the persecution of Catholics in the decades after the English Reformation in the sixteenth century. It now markets itself as 'one of the seven wonders of Wales'.

Brought back from the dead like Lazarus, Winifrede saw out her days living at the abbey at Gwytherin near Aberconwy, down the Pilgrim's Way, where she succeeded her aunt as abbess. Further along still, on the north coast of the Llyn Peninsula, is Beuno's base at Clynnog Fawr, from where he set out on his travels. The church is separated by a small stream from the chapel where Beuno was buried, and which in pre-Reformation times was a major pilgrimage shrine in its own right. Originally founded around 616, the main building of the church was rebuilt at the start of the sixteenth century to provide shelter, sustenance and a spiritual pick-me-up for those on the route.

Among those who played a major role in the revival of the North Wales Pilgrim's Way was Evelyn Davies, Anglican vicar of Aberdaron for eight years in the early 2000s. What had prompted her enthusiasm for the project, she explained shortly before her death in 2018, was the increase she had witnessed year-on-year in pilgrims turning up at her church asking how they could get across to Bardsey. 'Some were straightforward tourists, but many were not. Many were not necessarily, or even often, Christian, but they knew something was missing that was not to be found in the materialism that the world offers as a cure-all. So they had started looking outside, heard somewhere or read about Bardsey, and felt drawn to it. It had unlocked something in them that needed to find a way out.'[7] This sense of the pilgrimage infrastructure being re-established to respond to a quiet, largely unreported groundswell of interest is as much part of the story of the North Wales Pilgrim's Way as it is of the Camino in northern Spain.

Pilgrims on the final section of the Pilgrim's Way, also known as the Saints' Way because of the large number of small shrines to now obscure saints which line it, will be carrying their maps. But the closer they get to Aberdaron and Bardsey, the more likely they are also to have in their hands a collection of the poems of R. S. Thomas, who is the writer-in-residence on this route, even though he died in 2000 before it had been officially revived.[8] Thomas was nominated in his lifetime for the Nobel Prize for Literature for poetry that celebrates the landscape and traditions of North Wales, where he spent much of his life as an Anglican priest. His verse also responded to the silence and natural beauty of this sparsely populated countryside and found in it a way to approach an otherwise distant, hard-to-reach God. His poem about Bardsey, which opens and finishes this chapter, resonates with those who, like him, find themselves at journey's end on Bardsey Island.

Was the pilgrimage
I made to come to my own
self, to learn that, in times
like these, and for one like me,
God will never be plain and
out there, but dark rather, and
inexplicable, as though he were in here?[9]

CHAPTER EIGHT

KUMBH MELA
THE WORLD'S LARGEST PILGRIMAGE

※

*'It is difficult, if not impossible, to say to what extent
this kind of faith uplifts the soul.'*

MAHATMA GANDHI, ATTENDING KUMBH MELA IN 1915

In the *Mahabharata*, one of the seminal texts of Hinduism – with 100,000 couplets, sometimes referred to as the longest poem ever written – the story is told of Yudhishthira, a handsome, fair-skinned, lotus-eyed prince, born thanks to divine intervention after his mother, Queen Kunti, could not bear her husband, King Pandu, an heir. It is a moral tale about the human cost of jealousy and rivalry, in this case between Yudhishthira's clan, the Pandavas, and their royal cousins the Kauravas over control the kingdom of Kuru, the dominant political power in northern India around 1000 BCE.

Though he emerges victorious in the ensuing bloody struggle, Yudhishthira – described as a strong but humble man – is tormented by his deeds on the battlefield, especially the memory of his kin that he has slain. He seeks the counsel of two wise sages on how to make atonement. They send him on a pilgrimage. In the Sanskrit original of the *Mahabharata*, which covers a period from roughly the eleventh century BCE to the fourth CE, the word used for pilgrimage is *tirtha*, meaning a crossing, a ford or a bridge over a river. And it is to rivers – sacred in the Vedas, these holy texts that are the foundation stones of Hinduism – that Yudhishthira travels so as to make repentance for his sins and seek spiritual cleansing.

Accompanied on the route by a faithful dog, he reaches the end of his pilgrimage at the gate of heaven in the Himalayas (mountains are also regarded as sacred by Hindus). At this point, his four-legged friend turns out to be the god who is his birth father. Through divine intervention, Yudhishthira is reunited with his dead cousins, his self-abasement during his pilgrimage proving sufficient to bring them all back to the right moral path after the diversion of their earthly madness. It is the link between rivers and pilgrimage, though, that is most significant to our story.

Principal among the rivers that Yudhishthira visits on his *tirtha* is the Ganges (or Ganga), today regarded as a goddess in its own right by 1.1 billion Hindus (15 per cent of the world's population). He comes to its banks at Prayag, meaning 'place of sacrifice'. Later known as Allahabad and more recently as Prayagraj, it is today a city of over one million inhabitants in the northern Indian state of Uttar Pradesh. But, for Hindus, it is first and foremost a sacred place, mentioned in another ancient canonical text, the Rig Veda, as where Brahma, the creator god, performed the very first *yajna* – or sacrifice.

Prayag is where the Ganges meets the Yaruma as well as the mystical, invisible Sarasvati river, their confluence referred to as the *Triveni Sangam*. It is one of the four sites which, in a twelve-year cycle, host Kumbh Mela, the world's largest gathering of pilgrims by some distance, attracting 120 million in 2019. So huge was the crowd that this vast exodus of people could be seen from space, making it – according to headline writers at the time – 'the biggest show on earth'. Scale, it seems, is one distinguishing feature of Kumbh Mela among the world's great pilgrimages, but it is not everything, as the BBC's veteran India correspondent, Sir Mark Tully, reflected in his diary in 1989 after attending it. 'I had never been in such a peaceful crowd. There was no frenzy, just the calm certainty of faith; the knowledge that what had to be done had been done.'[1]

Alongside these two elements of size and faith, there is also an almost inexhaustible supply of head-turning, and occasionally head-spinning, spectacle. In the procession of pilgrim groups to the sacred river that can last all day, bejewelled elephants and holy cows with painted horns share a vivid canvas with an estimated 250,000 saffron-robed *sadhus* (monks, some with waist-length dreadlocks), full-bearded gurus, and ascetic *naga babas*, holy men who parade naked except for beads and yellow and orange garlands round their neck and a dusting of grey ash that gives their skin a phantom-like pallor. This covering is a sacred symbol and reminder that bodies may rot and burn, but there is a more enduring spiritual path to be sought that transcends death. And then, most eye-catching of all, there are the religious athletes, whose life of faith spurs them on to perform super-human acts of devotion and perseverance that go beyond their body's limits, squatting for hours, even days, or reputedly weeks, on one foot, or holding one withered arm permanently in the air in acts known as *tapaysa*, or spiritual discipline.

As a subcontinent and as a culture, India lends itself naturally to scale and spectacle – with 1.3 billion people, it is the world's largest democracy. Yet the scale and spectacle of Kumbh Mela aren't just about show. Attendance is not obligatory for Hindus, as *hajj* to Mecca is for Muslims, yet everyone aspires to be there at least once in a lifetime, even if that means walking for weeks or even months, on foot, from every corner of the country, and beyond. As an act, they believe, it is both meritorious and desirable, the ritual of bathing in the sacred river a chance to clean away sins from previous lives (Hindus believe in *samsara*, a cycle of birth, death and rebirth), and to achieve *moksha* – or liberation from *samsara* – which ushers in final union in the after-life with Brahman, the impersonal power beyond the universe. 'If a person, after committing a hundred bad sins,' states the *Mahabharata*, 'sprinkles himself with Ganges water, [it] burns all of them away as fire burns fuel'.

Then there is the chance to meet *sadhus*, who are everywhere to be seen at Kumbh Mela, even setting out their own stalls on the main procession routes. An audience with a *sadhu* is a chance to be inspired by them, their words and often their accompanying feats – lying on thorns is one popular display of spiritual prowess, as are walking on spikes and enduring extremes of hot and cold without flinching. Pilgrims can witness in such company how it is possible to go beyond bodily sensation and reach a place that is timeless.

Kumbh Mela itself is often described as timeless, or ageless. It conveys an aspiration that has seen it welcome an ever-rising tide of pilgrims from around the world in recent years. Numbers attending from overseas (including Hindus not living in India) were up 35 per cent in 2019 according to the *Times of India*. The non-Hindus among them are known to locals as *firangis* – or outsiders.

❊

The historical facts about Kumbh Mela are complicated, much debated and often plain obscure. For those who seek precision as well as spiritual sustenance, Yudhishthira's *tirtha* is one piece of the puzzle over the provenance of Kumbh Mela, revealing the early origins in Hinduism of the whole concept of pilgrimage, linked in with that of rituals of sacred bathing. Significant, too, in this heritage is the legend of good versus evil. The Sanskrit word *kumbh* is found in the Puranas, collections of myths that are another part of those core Vedic texts that are believed to date back over three millennia. It refers to a pot or pitcher that holds *amrit*, the nectar of immortality, drawn from a heavenly ocean of milk, located somewhere above the Himalayas. During a struggle between gods and demons, the ocean is churned up, causing the *kumbh* to be overturned. Drops of *amrit* spill and fall to earth at the four locations where Kumbh Mela now takes place: Prayag is one, and today the most attended of Kumbh Mela sites. A second, Haridwar, also on the Ganges in Uttarakhand, claims to be the oldest. Nashik on the banks of the river Godavari in Maharashtra, and Ujjain on the Shipra in Madhya Pradesh, make up the four.

The draw that sacred landscapes around the globe exert on the human spirit often rests on a combination of natural beauty interwoven with layer upon layer of memory, myth and association that has built up down the ages. Kumbh Mela is no exception. Its four sites, all next to rivers, have their own majesty even before tier after tier of tradition and tales and rituals are added in, the resulting combination being churned as the milky ocean in heaven was once churned. What has emerged is something powerfully other.

At both Haridwar and Prayag, a full Kumbh Mela takes place every twelve years, usually during the first three months of the year, with Ardh (or half) Kumbh after six years. Every 144 years, Prayag holds 'Great' Kumbh Mela, the most recent having been in 2001. Kumbhs at Nashik and Ujjain slot into this calendar, so that there is no overlap, to complete the overall twelve-year cycle, with each site timing its celebration around a set of astrological calculations based on the positions of the sun, the moon and Jupiter. (The word *kumbh* also appears as the Hindi word for Aquarius, the astrological sign in which Jupiter resides during the Haridwar Mela.)

As to the antiquity of Kumbhs, again there is little firm agreement but a broad consensus that these extraordinary events have been happening for around 1,300 years, even if not under the name of Kumbh Mela. One popular version of their emergence credits the eighth-century Hindu philosopher Adi Shankara, founder of four major monasteries, who instituted regular gatherings of monks and ascetics for discussion and debate. It was part of his more general push to bring order and coherence to the many different schools of thought to be found within Hinduism.

However, it was only really in the late eighteenth and nineteenth century, during British rule in India, that the phrase Kumbh Mela is first recorded to describe such gatherings. The component words, of course, have a longer vintage – the *kumbh* found in the story of the spilt nectar (though with no mention in the sacred texts of any sort of accompanying festival), and the *mela* as a fair or assembly. Many places in India had and still have their own local fairs called *magha* or *mahar mela*. The Magha Mela festival in Tamil Nadu, in southern India, for example, attracts millions.

Such mela have certainly been taking place in India for centuries, including at the four locations of today's Kumbh Mela. And these mela have long had (alongside commercial aspects) a religious element that includes ritual bathing in holy waters, sometimes called *tithra* bathing. The early Hindu texts provide an abundance of detail about *snana*, or bathing, as a regular religious observance. In the Puranas, bathing in rivers is referred to repeatedly as an easy, cheap, open-to-all-regardless-of-means-or-status alternative to elaborate, hierarchical temple ceremonies. And so ritual bathing in the sacred rivers at the four cities that now host Kumbh Mela becomes both an inner and an outer pilgrimage. The outer part lies in the journey to get there, and communal activities on arrival, including the walking into the water of the river, which is what the outside world sees. The inner aspect is immersion in the water as a private, personal ritual of cleansing the eternal soul.

Religious bathing rituals at Prayag are described as early as the middle years of the seventh century CE by Xuan Zang, a Chinese Buddhist monk who spent seventeen years journeying in India during the T'ang dynasty. As well as the city's temples and palaces, he writes in his *Record of the Western Regions* of how people would go into the water at the junction of the great rivers and immerse themselves. There is some dispute, though, as to whether what he describes was a Hindu or a Buddhist ritual, since most of his travel memoir concerned Buddhist shrines. Other accounts of Prayag at the end of the first millennium also speak of pilgrims gathering there but add detail to the picture in the shape of accompanying vendors, monks and guides. None refers to the assembly as Kumbh Mela.

For the first, widely accepted references to Kumbh Mela, we have to fast-forward to the end of the eighteenth century and the published account of one Captain Thomas Hardwicke of the British East India Company, who served in the Bengal Artillery, part of the 260,000-strong private army that underpinned its control of India. In 1796, he found himself in the Himalayan foothills at Haridwar – the city's name means 'Gateway to the Gods'. He reports on its annual fair and market (or mela) that, once every twelve years, he stated, became a Kumbh Mela. He estimates the numbers of pilgrims arriving at around two and a half million. They were there to take part not just in the bathing rituals and religious processions, but also in – to Hardwicke's eyes – the equally significant trading and political dimensions of the gathering. In his account, colourfully dressed monks rub shoulders amid chaotic scenes with merchants who have travelled to sell their wares not just from the whole Indian subcontinent but also from further afield.[2] Commerce and worship coexist seamlessly. It was the former that drew Hardwicke's employers, the British East India Company, into doing more than simply policing and observing the Haridwar mela. They spotted the possibility of exploiting its trading and tax-raising potential – and, ultimately, that of what emerged as the other three Kumbh Mela cities.

Pursuit of profit came at a price, however, because it also meant exercising some sort of crowd control at these Kumbh Mela, without standing on the toes of those who traditionally ran them, the *akharas*. Hardwicke gives chapter and verse on these monkish bands, part religious order, part performance troop, and part quasi-military, their origins being as defenders of large, notable monasteries from attackers. On the streets of Haridwar, in their colour-coded regalia, they cut a dash in the great set-piece processions of Kumbh Mela, but they were also prone, he observed, to bitter rivalries and hence to outbreaks of violence. In the year of Hardwicke's visit, at least 500 pilgrims were killed in battles that broke out between the various *akharas*. And it wasn't an isolated spasm of brutality. At the Nashik mela in 1690, 60,000 pilgrims are reported to have died as a result of clashes over which *akhara* could bathe first in the sacred river.

Diplomacy and deployment of its own military might saw the East India Company defuse such tensions. It brought a bureaucratic order of sorts to the gatherings, while all the time avoiding a heavy hand that would offend pilgrim sensitivities and reduce potential revenue. Kumbh Mela, though, was never ultimately something they could control. Yet they left their mark. Some would even go so far as to say that it was the East India Company that invented Kumbh Mela as a 'brand'.

That, though, would be to sideline the *akharas*, who had already shown themselves as capable of organization as they were of outbursts of violent rivalry. By the eighteenth century, they had formed themselves into an accepted pattern of thirteen clans. Of these, ten were Hindu – divided seven to three between Shaivas (their focus being on the god Shiva) and Vaishnavas (on Vishnu) – and three Sikh. Sometimes referred to as a sect of Hinduism, Sikhism is more properly a body of beliefs, founded at the end of the fifteenth century in India by Guru Nanak, drawing on both Hindu and Islamic sources, as well as distinctive ideas and practices.

Yet it is equally true that with the involvement of the British, Kumbh Mela on the whole became in the early decades of the nineteenth century both more prosperous and more peaceful events (though not infallibly, with a stampede at Haridwar in 1820 killing 485). Protocols were agreed and put in place to avoid clashes over which *akharas* had precedence, allowing their monks to become less militant and more spiritual. The balance, though, remained fragile. When India rose in rebellion against the British in 1857, a finger of blame was pointed at Kumbh Mela, where the colonial power believed nationalist sentiments had been spreading among pilgrims who then carried them back to their home states. Once the uprising had been suppressed, the British Raj took over control from the East India Company.

✦

Though Kumbh Mela is self-avowedly timeless, it can also get entangled in time-limited events. After Indian independence in 1947, numbers attending grew steadily as the nation's confidence in itself rose, from five million in the 1950s, to fifteen million by 1989, forty million in one single day in 2001, and 120 million in 2019. The independence leader Mahatma Gandhi understood the importance of Kumbh Mela, travelling to Haridwar in 1915 soon after he returned to his birthplace from working as a lawyer in South Africa. In the 1930s, during the struggle to end colonial rule, Jawaharlal Nehru, the man who went on to become India's first post-independence prime minister, made a point of attending the Prayag Kumbh. And both Gandhi and Nehru left instructions on their deaths that a part of their ashes be scattered at the *sangram* there.

Politicians have continued since to attend Kumbh Mela. Nehru's daughter, Indira Gandhi, was there in 1977, around election time. So was his granddaughter-in-law, Sonia Gandhi, in 2001, again as polling day approached. Each woman wanted to show pilgrims – and Indian voters, looking on via the media – that, by attending Kumbh Mela, they understood and were part of Indian culture (especially important in the case of Sonia Gandhi, as the Italian-born widow of Rajiv Gandhi, assassinated in 1991, leaving her reluctantly to take on the mantle of leadership of the Congress Party).

There are, by tradition, up to six principal bathing days at each Kumbh Mela. But on most days, during the roughly fifty that make up the festival, bathers will start coming down to the river from dawn, heading for the *ghats*, or bathing spots. (One at Haridwar claims to have a footprint left by the god Vishnu on one of its steps.) On the most auspicious days, as they are called, which often coincide with the full moon, that trickle at sunrise quickly becomes a human torrent as the *akharas* – in their agreed order – process through the waiting crowds with their banners and flags flying, some in regimented formation, others accompanied by elephants, camels and horses, chariots and tractors towing floats. Stewards and police struggle to keep order. For those who have travelled far, often from remote rural villages, the challenge in this vast melee is simply to take it all in as they cling close to their families, even to the point sometimes of binding themselves to each other with string or rope. Each Kumbh Mela sees thousands of children and aunts and grandfathers get separated in the crush, only to be reunited later in the day after the lost-and-found tannoy announcements that are a constant background hum.

Men and women head for separate *ghats*, partitioned off by bamboo barricades. Once at the water's edge, some men run straight in, splashing with the exuberance of finally being there. Others are more tentative, seeking out space where there is usually none for a moment's quiet prayer. A swami (religious teacher) stands disrobing among the already discarded shoes and clothing of others, while a helper holds a gold-coloured umbrella over his head. For modesty reasons, the women go into the water in their saris, drying them later like kites in the breeze. The men strip down to underwear, or go further, some clutching whatever modesty cloth they had been wearing above the heads to keep it dry. Others will have their heads shaved before they enter the water, but most simply dip under, hair and all, and then resurface to offer a prayer as the remaining drops trickle through their hands, extended in prayer, or are wiped away from their heads and faces.

Some will swim a few strokes, but space – especially on these high days – is short. Meanwhile, guards hover, either submerged up to their shoulders, the word Police on the back of their shirts just visible above the water, or further out in boats, in case any bathers get swept away, and the chain railings that have been put in place to catch them prove insufficient. Some bathers go in as a group, accompanied by a priest, who will lead the prayers, including to ancestors, and make offerings to the river goddess of flowers, milk or coconut. Those wanting a liquid keepsake of Kumbh Mela scoop up Ganges water in brass *puja* pots, just as Christian pilgrims fill their Virgin Mary-shaped bottles with holy water at Lourdes. As they clamber out of the water, back into the landslide of humanity on the shore, pilgrims are herded away as quickly as possible, to make way for more to take their place. Millions can bathe in the river on a single day.

If the *snana* is over in a few minutes, it is nonetheless for some the summit of a lifetime's devotion and yearning. But, as with other pilgrimages, the journey to the river can be as important as the final destination. For every young city dweller who comes for a single day on the hundreds of extra trains that are laid on for each Kumbh Mela, grabbing an e-rickshaw at the station, there are the *kalpavasis*, an older generation of pilgrims who are the first to arrive and the last to leave Kumbh Mela over its whole fifty-day span. They are up at dawn in time for a bathe at six each morning, often the first of three dips, which is followed by a simple meal. The rest of the day is spent in prayer and meditation. In life's final furlong, the *kalpavasis* want only to commit themselves more and more to the gods. Once they have attended twelve successive Kumbhs, they can go through a religious ceremony known as *shayya daan* ('donating the bed') that has been likened to attending their own funeral. And then there are those, mixed in with the crowds, who have walked all the way, with their few possessions bound up and carried on their heads, sometimes barefoot, for hundreds of kilometres to be at Kumbh Mela.

If the means and journey times of pilgrims vary greatly, what starts out as a seemingly endless number of self-selected cohesive groups, each made up of those with similar backgrounds, outlooks and – arguably more in the past than today – from the same caste, soon find themselves on arrival in a huge melting pot. That is the point of Kumbh Mela. It brings all Hindus together, whatever their personal belief in a religion that has many aspects, and many gods, and is so flexible in accommodating them all that very little ever counts as heresy. At Kumbh Mela, for once, everyone in attendance is on shared ground – literally and theologically. Divisions are attenuated – despite the presence of politicians trying to woo voters – and what emerges above all is a single Hindu practice.

For the day-trippers, trains are there to take them home afterwards, but for most pilgrims – including *firangis* from overseas who can now book luxury billets in the vast tented village that is put up for the festival – the experience is not just about showpiece rituals but also about communal living for however many days they are part of this enormous brother- and sisterhood. Away from the main processions, *ghats* and the thousands of vendors who treat Kumbh as one big market, every conceivable entertainment is available, ancient and modern, from devotional singing to laser light shows, classical dance to fireworks. The noise levels at Kumbh Mela rarely subside when so many people are in one place, whether it be piped music, both sacred and from Bollywood, or broadcast pitches by the multitude of religious men and the occasional woman who have come to put across their religious messages to such a large captive audience.

In the tent city, in the various compounds of each of the *akharas*, some of them with impressive entrances made out of temple façades painted onto cloth and held up by wooden scaffolding, recruitment and initiation rites take place. Elsewhere *sadhus* sit cross-legged in front of burning fire pits dispensing wisdom to pilgrims. So, too, do *naga babas*, though often through a distinctive fug of marijuana. There are even now occasional *sadhvi* – or female *sadhu* – as Hinduism adapts to changes in the wider society of which it is an integral part. Kumbh Mela in 2019 saw another step towards modern inclusivity and tolerance when one of the *akhara* compounds played host to a group that calls itself Kinnar Akhara, made up of mainly transgender women, who in their assembly tent put on a well-received programme of performances, discussions and readings.

Back at the river banks in the evenings, the rituals continue, with blessings – *aartis* – offered every night by priests on plinths next to the water, accompanied by a fire purification ceremony to honour the gods that recalls the first ever such sacrifice by Brahma as recounted in the Rig Veda. Beyond them, out on the river, small banana-leaf coracles float by cradling tea lights, like a passing fleet of glowworms.

CHAPTER NINE

THE BUDDHA TRAIL
THE PERIPATETIC
PILGRIM

☀

*'It is in Bodh Gaya that the traveller will find something
to equal the object of his pilgrimage.'*

JEET THAYIL, INDIAN POET AND NOVELIST[1]

Each morning, at dawn, before pilgrims arrive in their coaches, a rag-tag army of local children are busy under the sprawling branches of the giant, banyan tree at Bodh Gaya. Known to the world's 550 million Buddhists as the Bodhi Tree, it is said to be the place where the Buddha first achieved enlightenment 2,500 years ago. In his subsequent writings, he directed his followers to come here to find inspiration in their lives, but these local youngsters' motives are more earthy. Bihar, the state in which Bodh Gaya is located, is one of India's poorest. They are scrambling on the ground to gather any leaves that have fallen overnight, which can then be sold to the visitors who come to seek serenity in the Buddha's footsteps.

During opening hours, the tree is perpetually encircled by three impenetrable concentric rings. Working outwards, first there is the tall brick wall that stops too-eager hands from clawing away at bits of its trunk. Next come the security guards who prevent the more determined pilgrims from snapping off twigs that will be more relic than souvenir when they get it back home. And finally, there is the crowd of visitors who gather round as part of immersing themselves in the whole complex at Bodh Gaya. They will have stepped inside the elaborately carved, pyramidal, sixth-century CE colossus of the Mahabodhi Temple, and been awe-struck in front of the much more recent (1989) 25-metre tall statue of the 'Great Buddha'. Above all, though, they will want to stand in the shadow of a tree that is the centrepiece of the holiest site in world Buddhism.

At this early hour, with the sky still a lemony pink, such obstacles have yet to appear. So the children have free rein to pick up and bag any leaves they can find. Clear plastic envelopes, containing a single leaf from what is arguably the most famous tree in the world command quite a premium as licit relics among the estimated two million pilgrims who come here each year. The foreigners are reputedly the most susceptible, many of them Buddhists from Southeast Asian countries on a once-in-a-lifetime pilgrimage on the 'Buddha Trail'. It consists, depending on the length of their itinerary, of a circuit of four major sites (Bodh Gaya being the principal among them), plus – for those with more time and resources – four minor ones. Among overseas visitors coming to India each year, an estimated 7 per cent arrive on such Buddhist pilgrimages.

Quite what the Buddha himself would make of it all is hard to decide. Throughout his life, he pointedly and repeatedly shrugged off any cult of personality. It was not, he stressed to his *bhikkhus* (disciples, now used to mean monks and nuns), all about him, where he went, or the events of his life, but rather his teachings about *dhamma*, 'right life', which he described as a path of great antiquity towards enlightenment that had been travelled by human beings long before him. Under the Bodhi Tree – which in Pali, the ancient dialect of this part of northern India, means 'the tree of enlightenment' – he had reached a serene understanding about the fundamental truths of the cosmos that shaped every creature in it. It was this knowledge that liberated him from the usual human concerns about ego, possessions, suffering and death.

Even accounts in the Buddhist scriptures – notably the *Nidana-katha*, a collection of stories about the Buddha – seem to want to distract attention away from there being an actual Bodhi Tree. They emphasize how the earth had shuddered around the original tree as the Buddha approached the moment of enlightenment, 'as though it was a huge cartwheel lying on its hub, and somebody was treading on its rim'.[2] The sacred texts make abundantly clear this was no ordinary tree, but instead a manifestation of the invisible power at work in the universe, roughly like the 'world-tree' in the Garden of Eden in the Judeo-Christian creation myth.

So how has this actual tree, not even the original to stand on the spot, but reputedly the fourth-generation of a series of saplings grown from the first Bodhi Tree, re-imported into India from Sri Lanka at the end of the nineteenth century, achieved such an elevated status among Buddhists that its leaves alone can keep in food the families of the youngsters who gather them? In the simplest of terms, it is because the Buddha told people to go there. He may not have been keen on a personality cult focused on himself, but he was an unabashed fan of pilgrimage. In the *Mahaparinibbana Sutta*, which describes the Buddha's death, he unambiguously urges his devotees to make pilgrimage as part of their own search for enlightenment.

The request chimes with the precious few biographical details that we know about him – and even these are, historians argue, at best provisional. The standard story is that, in 594 BCE in Kapilavat-thu, northern India, just inside the border of what is now Nepal, 29-year-old Siddhartha Gotama turned his back on his princely family and his life of luxury (thirty-two nursemaids, by some largely imagined accounts, on hand in the palaces he inhabited to attend on him). He was also abandoning his wife and recently born son, then as now a powerfully counter-cultural act, but Gotama headed out nonetheless through what is referred to as the Great Renunciation Gate. In the yellow robes of a monk, he wandered the forests of the vast Gangetic Plains, starving himself, doing yoga, and pushing his hitherto pampered, plump body to its very limits in an effort to carry himself beyond the cares and needs of the physical universe. With only a begging bowl to sustain himself, he was on a pilgrim journey, some of the time alone, others with a small group of like-minded ascetics.

After six years of hardship, and despairing that he would ever reach his goal, he left behind his colleagues and sat down one spring day under the Bodhi Tree and that yearned-for moment of enlightenment finally came. For the next forty-five years, the Buddha continued to wander, now more often than not accom-panied by a crowd of acolytes who wanted – literally and spiritu-ally – to follow the path he had trodden. Right up to his death at the age of 80, he taught all those who would listen about how to achieve liberation from what he described as a wheel of suffering that binds humankind.

Bodh Gaya, as well as the other three main shrines that appear in the biography – Lumbini, where he was born, Sarnath, where he gave his first sermon, and Kusinagara, where he died – were all places, he is recorded as saying in the scriptures, that 'a pious man should visit and look upon with feelings of reverence'. Moreover, he remarks to Ananda, the closest of the group that accompanied him after his enlightenment, that those on such a pilgrimage who die en route ('the breaking up of the body') will be reborn in Nibbana, or Nirvana, the 'realm of heavenly happiness'. There is but one proviso: their hearts must be 'stablished in faith'.

Thus the pilgrim has a special status in Buddhism. Temporarily or permanently, they are called to abandon the world to seek something more. Their mission cannot be confused with mere sightseeing. It is an intention to achieve a wholesome mental state. This is done by following the Buddha's instructions about 'right thought, right speech, right action'. In the Buddhist scriptures, there is active encouragement to become a 'wanderer', liberated from all worldly attachments, either all alone, or as a member of the Buddha's followers – the *Sangha* (community) of enlightened ones. 'Go ye *bhikkhus*,' instructs the *Mahavagga*, a compilation of the stories of the Buddha agreed around 400 BCE by the First Council of monks held after his death, 'wander for the gain of the many, for the welfare of the many, [and] out of compassion for the world'.

Through the wandering lives of monks, without a settled home, but intent on teaching what is sometimes today called mindfulness, Buddhism spread rapidly throughout the Indian subcontinent and further afield. Present-day pilgrims, though, return to the earthly source of it all not on foot (save for a handful of zealots) but in coaches and trains. Logic suggests that they should start at Lumbini, 20 kilometres from Nepal's border with India, as the Buddha's birthplace, and then head on an anti-clockwise 1,000-kilometre circuit via Sarnath, close to the city of Varanasi, and then Bodh Gaya (though they come in reverse order), ending up at Kusinagara in Uttar Pradesh where he died. But geography and infrastructure, too, have a part to play. Bodh Gaya is the only one of the four to have its own airport and it is the most popular – and for some time-poor pilgrims their only – destination. At

Lumbini, researchers have dug down into the nationalities most heavily represented among those 1.5 million visitors who come there during the peak pilgrim season that runs from October to March (avoiding the monsoons). South and Southeastern Asian countries with sizeable Buddhist populations dominate the top ten – Sri Lanka, Thailand, Burma (Myanmar), Vietnam, China, Vietnam, South Korea and Japan. Only Germany and France, among Western nations, merit a mention.

One of the peculiarities of the Buddha Trail is that home-grown Indian Buddhists are not, as might be expected, the dominant group. 'Domestic' visitors account for around three-quarters of the numbers. Yet Buddhism makes up at most 2 per cent of the Indian population. Many of the Indian pilgrims will be Hindus, the demarcation between their faith and Buddhism blurred, with shared beliefs in *dhamma* and reincarnation, but differences on the role of a creator god and the caste system.

That the cradle of the fourth-largest global faith should be in a country where its followers are a tiny minority is unusual in the story of world pilgrimage but reflects the troubled history of Buddhism on Indian soil. After it had been exported across Asia (it remains the majority faith in Cambodia, Thailand, Burma and Sri Lanka), it was wiped out in India from the thirteenth to nineteenth centuries, leaving it to British colonialists to 'rediscover' its great shrines. Some had been left to rot, while Bodh Gaya, and the Bodhi Tree, had been subsumed into Hinduism. Today's Buddha Trail, then, is both ancient and modern.

✲

If the Buddha is the inspiration for the trail that carries his name, then the one who arguably brought it all together as a whole in a practical sense was Ashoka the Great, third and greatest ruler of the Maurya Empire. Under his leadership from 268 to 232 BCE, it spread out over almost the entire Indian subcontinent. His early years on the throne were taken up with war in Kalinga (modern-day Orissa state) but, once victorious, he repented of bloodshed and embraced the Buddhist goal of *dhamma* as his guiding principle. This meant, in the public arena, building public utilities such as wells and hospitals. In his own life, too, he was a great evangelist for Buddhism, even sending his son and daughter as missionaries to Sri Lanka. Within his realm he followed the Buddha's dictate on places to be 'looked upon with feelings of reverence' and travelled to each of the four sites most associated with his legacy.

The infrastructure that Ashoka left behind on his own pilgrimage remains to this day, his enthusiasm for building on a great scale in stone something he had learnt from the Greeks, and Alexander the Great in particular. By some accounts Ashoka commissioned 84,000 temples and *stupas* (commemorative burial mounds) around his empire, and it is even claimed that he entrusted to each a portion of the Buddha's ashes. It is for his pillars that he is perhaps best remembered today. These were not just monuments to his power and piety. They also had a teaching purpose, being inscribed with edicts that purport to be the emperor's understanding of what a good Buddhist – and hence a good ruler and subject – should do.

In the centuries when Buddhism was eclipsed in India, these pillars of polished sandstone, topped by exquisitely carved capitals, were thought lost, but were rediscovered in late nineteenth-century excavations. The example at Lumbini refers in its inscription to Ashoka in the third person as having worshipped on the spot because the Buddha had been born there. '(He) both caused to be made a stone bearing a horse and caused a stone pillar to be set up [in order to show] that the Blessed One was born here. [He] made the village of Lumbini free of taxes, and paying [only] an eighth share [of the produce].'

That use of the third person, though not unprecedented in naming monarchs and emperors as part of the aura they created around themselves, has led some subsequently to suggest that Lumbini's pillar was put up many centuries after Ashoka had travelled there. It is certainly known to have been in place in the seventh century CE, when the Chinese Buddhist monk Xuan Zang (who we have already met in Prayag) came to Lumbini on his travels and records both the horse sculpture on the capital and the pillar, by that time broken in two. He makes, though, no mention of any inscription, adding to speculation that it came later still.

Ashoka also went to Bodh Gaya, which in his day was known as Bodhimanda ('ground around the Bodhi Tree') or Sambodhi, only getting its present name in the eighteenth century. And at Kusinagara, the remains of a mighty *stupa* he commissioned can still be seen. It is, however, the Ashokean pillar at Sarnath that has the greatest significance for modern-day India, the four Asiatic lions on the capital that topped it now the emblem of the whole nation. They were unearthed in the winter of 1904 during excavations at the site, the base still standing on what is thought to be its original site, but the pillar broken into three parts. It had been, archaeologists are convinced, deliberately destroyed at an unknown date, along with the carved 32-spoke 'Wheel of Dhamma' that once crowned the entire capital. Only fragments of it survived. The rest of the capital, however, was well-preserved, and was immediately transferred to a museum set up at Sarnath.

The lion was frequently used in Buddhism to represent the Buddha himself, while the position of the four lions, back-to-back and facing out, has been variously interpreted as symbolizing the four points of the compass of Ashoka's empire, the spread of Buddhism far and wide, or the Four Noble Truths that the Buddha taught.

Among Ashoka's other bequests is believed to be the foundation of the once powerful Buddhist university at Nalanda, near Rajgir in Bihar state, then capital of the Maurya Empire (and today one of the second group of four pilgrim sites on the Buddha Trail because of the legend of the angry elephant, which he calmed mid-charge through love and compassion). Now in ruins, excavations have located a *stupa* from the fifth century BCE, backing up the claim that the Buddha himself came to Nalanda and taught monks in a mango grove. In its heyday, as many as 10,000 would be studying at any one time, but by 1200 CE it had been reduced to ruins.

Not only did Ashoka establish a precedent for the modern pilgrim by visiting the sites on the Buddha trail, he also encouraged his court officials to go there too, so that they might administer justice in a more ethical way. After his death, even as his empire crumbled, the itinerary Ashoka had followed continued to be popular with pilgrims, who travelled from as far afield as Tibet and China, often on foot, across the Takla Makan desert, through the windswept passes in the Pamir and Hindu Kush mountain ranges, returning home with tales of a thriving monastic and scholarly culture in the region where the Buddha had once taught.

Quite how that culture was wiped out, with the result that Buddhism itself was ghosted away from the land of its birth to flourish in what had once been missionary lands, remains a matter of debate. What is common to most accounts is the defencelessness of those Buddhists at the great monasteries and shrines. They couldn't withstand the assault of Turkic Muslim invaders from Central Asia in the early decades of the sixth century CE, led by a king, Mihirakula, who is described in Buddhist texts as brutal, barbaric and an avowed enemy of Buddhists. A century later, the Chinese Buddhist monk Xuan Zang records on his travels that Mihirakula had destroyed monasteries and shrines, leaving behind him (when he was finally vanquished by Indian princes) a much-reduced Buddhist patrimony in the region. It did manage to revive itself, but when the war-like Muslim Mughals came in the thirteenth century, a precursor to later invasions, this time it was utterly obliterated, with thousands of monks beheaded, their books burned (and with them documentary evidence of Buddhism's history) and temples, pillars and *stupas* reduced to rubble.

As pacifists, it has been suggested, the custodians of the Buddha's legacy in northern India may simply have been unwilling to engage in combat with their attackers, even if it cost them every earthly thing. But they may also, according to some accounts, have lost the trust and loyalty of the local population, who failed to rally to their defence in the face of the onslaught by outsiders. This was because the people had come to regard the monasteries as bloated on power, and the monks corrupt in their practices and complacent over the loyalty of those who lived under their authority. In the wake of the invasion, with any surviving Buddhist monks and priests having fled, they transferred their faith allegiance easily, and repurposed remaining places of worship appropriately.

Many of the great Buddhist sites, though, were left to rot. Even today, farmers in Bihar regularly plough up scattered stone effigies that once stood in monasteries and temples as hallowed representations of the Buddha. *Stupas* that had been torn down became a ready source of bricks to be reused in building homes. At Bodh Gaya, which in the Buddha's time would have welcomed Hindu visitors without a second glance, control passed to Hindu priests. A Tibetan traveller in 1234 reported that only four Buddhist monks remained. Later visitors report a Hindu chief priest or Mahant as being in charge. That remained the situation in 1886, when under the British Raj the English poet and journalist Edwin Arnold came to Bodh Gaya. He asked his Hindu hosts if he could pick a leaf from the Bodhi Tree. They replied, he reported, 'pluck as many as you like ... it is nought to us'. In his report of the exchange, Arnold railed at what he perceived as wilful neglect of the Buddhist relics by the Hindu priest in what for him should rightfully be regarded as 'the Mecca, the Jerusalem, of a million Oriental congregations'.[3]

After six centuries of oblivion, it was British archaeologists in the nineteenth century who uncovered the Indian roots of Buddhism, ultimately leading to the reopening of the Buddha Trail. In 1837, Alexander Cunningham carried out excavations at Sarnath and prepared detailed drawings of what he had found buried there to argue for its importance in the Buddha's life. Five years later, he did the same at Sankassa (another of the second group of four sites associated with the Buddha on the modern-day pilgrim trail). And then in 1854, drawing on the eyewitness accounts of earlier visitors such as Xuan Zang, Cunningham published *The Bhilsa Topes*, where he set out for a new age the story of the Buddha and the rise of Buddhism in India.

Cunningham worked closely with Indian scholars. In the closing decades of the nineteenth century, nourished by the evidence presented in his books, a home-grown Buddhist revival got underway, spearheaded above all by Anagarika Dharmapala. Born in Buddhist Sri Lanka, he was inspired to visit Bodh Gaya for the first time in 1885 by reading Edwin Arnold's account. Returning in 1892 to see the newly restored (by the British authorities) Mahabodhi Temple there, he was upset that it remained in the hands of Hindu priests, and so established the Mahabodhi Society in Calcutta to campaign for Buddhists to have an equal say in its day-to-day management. It proved a lengthy legal battle, resolved only after his death at Sarnath in 1933, but in the process his society became a powerhouse for promoting the role of Buddhism in the history of India – and in its present-day incarnation. Dharmapala played a major role, in particular, in restoring the fourth of the main Buddha Trail sites, at Kusinagara where the Buddha died, and turning what had been a neglected ruin into a place capable of inspiring pilgrims once again.

※

At Lumbini, as at Bodh Gaya, the day begins early. The first sign of life, however, is not children on the make around a Bodhi Tree (though Lumbini has one, as do all the other major Buddha Trail sites, cuttings of cuttings of cuttings of the original). Instead what disturbs the sleepy atmosphere of this still rural town is the shrine's very own dawn chorus. The sound of drums and bells mixes with the chanting in Pali of passages from the Buddhist scriptures. A procession of pilgrims is underway, the prayer flags favoured by Tibetan Buddhists adding a vivid splash of colour, as do the monks' claret robes. After passing over a small canal, it wends its way past the crumbling ruins of Buddhist *viharas* (monasteries) that date from the third century BCE to the fifth century CE, and then skirts the edge of the *Pushkarini*, or sacred pool where Queen Maya is said, 2,500 years ago, to have taken a ritual bath shortly before giving birth to Siddhartha Gotama in a grove of Sala trees. The pilgrims' final destination is the simple, white-walled Maya Devi Temple, which stands on what is claimed as the exact spot of the Buddha's delivery into this world. In legend, he was born talking, his first words being, 'this is my last birth'.

Inside the temple, there are scenes taken from the Buddha's biography painted onto the walls. His stated wish for the focus not to fall on him, but rather on his teachings, once again proves hard to honour. 'He who sees me, sees the *dhamma*,' he once remarked, 'and he who sees the *dhamma* sees me'. For his part, the Buddha saw himself as a guide, teacher and even exemplar, but arguably not a god – though this interpretation is disputed by the various schools within Buddhism that have grown up over the millennia. For some, Siddhartha Gotama was the twenty-eighth in a line of Buddhas, a name given to supremely enlightened beings of whom there can only be one in the universe in any given period. Those who today accept his place in that succession look forward to the coming of the twenty-ninth Buddha but understand that it may be many thousands of years before it happens.

There are, within Buddhism, many ways to venerate the twenty-eighth Buddha: by sitting still, perhaps under a tree, and meditating on his qualities; by reading the scriptures; by honouring a figure of him; or by making offerings. All are held to foster the sort of spiritual discipline he advocated. At Lumbini, however, there is that special sense – present elsewhere on the trail, too – that pilgrims are retracing his steps. They do this despite knowing that any attachment to a definitive life story of the Buddha is, as the distinguished religious writer Karen Armstrong puts it, 'a very un-Buddhist thing [because] no authority should be revered, however august; Buddhists must motivate themselves and rely on their own effort, not on a charismatic leader'.[4] Yet the pilgrims are able to accommodate more than one approach to belief simultaneously, as the rise in their numbers in northern India and Nepal in recent times testifies. Lumbini in particular received a significant boost in 2013 when archaeologists dug down underneath the Maya Devi Temple and found not only the remains of the shrine that Ashoka had built during his time in Lumbini, but also directly underneath it an even older timber structure. Carbon-dating has suggested that this hitherto unknown formation existed even before the Ashokean shrine, maybe as an open-air enclosure or altar, potentially including a tree of enlightenment, which might make it the earliest surviving Buddhist site in the world. The facts, once again, are disputed, with some archaeological experts arguing that the 'discovery' could simply be a nature shrine, focused on tree worship.

Among the Buddhist monks who travelled to Lumbini in its early centuries as a pilgrim site, the appeal was in part to experience the world as the Buddha would have experienced it as he started off on his own pilgrimage towards enlightenment. Back then it remained a poor and isolated part of the world that stood outside time. And, for twenty-first-century visitors, that spirit remains alive, not just because recent excavations potentially carry them back 2,500 years, but also because the custodians deliberately set the clocks fifteen minutes adrift of the surrounding region. Their aim is to create for pilgrims – sometimes on tight timetables to get round the circuit between the four shrines – an extra pocket of space where the insistent demands of the outside world can briefly be ignored and spiritual imperatives pursued.

The dawn procession is continuing its progress. In front of Lumbini's version of the Bodhi Tree, pilgrims are falling to the ground in full prostration, then rising up to standing and repeating the movement time and again. It is a ritual they undertake to achieve mindfulness, that most sought-after of qualities in today's Western world, by being more grounded, which in turn releases the individual from the grip of ego. As the group move on, among the ruins, some pause before *stupas* to lay offerings, light candles and incense sticks and bow their heads in prayer. When they visit taller *stupas* elsewhere on the trail, some throw up weighted slings of white silk in an effort to attach their offering to the rounded upper part of the structure, where it will sit like a strange outcrop.

After Lumbini, in the geography of the trail, comes Sarnath, where legend suggests the Buddha delivered his very first sermon in what was then a deer park at Isipathana, a place favoured by ancient sages for meditation. It was two months after he had achieved enlightenment and he had come to meet the same five monks with whom he had parted company before he headed to Bodh Gaya. They had gone their separate ways because the Buddha rejected their extreme asceticism in favour of what he called 'a middle way'. The reunion, then, was not guaranteed to be a happy or harmonious one, but his 'Discourse on Turning the Wheel of Dhamma' convinced them to become the first members of the *Sangha* – or community of enlightened ones – who followed him.

Subsequently, according to the biography that many Buddhists accept, he would return to Sarnath from his wanderings to sit out the monsoon season in the Mulagandhakuti Vihara, in front of which later was to stand Sarnath's now celebrated Ashokean pillar. The monastery was destroyed by the thirteenth-century invaders, but in the 1930s Anagarika Dharmapala's Mahabodhi Society built a new temple on the same spot.

After Bodh Gaya, the final stopping place on the essential pilgrimage is Kusinagara, small in scale in comparison to what has gone before, but where the Buddha, with his disciple Ananda at his side, died and attained *parinibbana*, the final stage of Nibbana. 'The Place of the Great Passing Away', as it is known, counts as its prized object the Reclining Buddha, 3.5 metres long, cut from a single piece of stone, covered in gold leaf. It represents the Enlightened One on his deathbed and, unlike most representations where he sits crossed in the lotus position, he is resting on his right side.

Travelling with his companion, Ananda, the Buddha had a premonition of his earthly life drawing to an end and had been heading for Lumbini, when he could go no further. Ananda made him a bed next to the Hiranyavati River, between two trees, with its head facing north. 'The nature of things dictates that we must leave those dear to us', the Buddha told him. 'Everything born contains its own cessation. I too, am grown old, and full of years, my journey is drawing to its close.'

An inscription in the Parinibbana Stupa, which contains the Reclining Buddha, dates the sculptured figure to the fifth century CE, commissioned by the Hindu rulers of the Gupta Empire, for whom Kusinagara was a major centre. Once again there is that interchange between Hindus and Buddhists. Yet it was only rediscovered in 1876 by the British archaeologist A. C. L. Carlleyle. Its many scattered fragments had to be painstakingly pieced together.

Some present-day pilgrims will gather to re-enact a ritual carried out by his closest circle 2,500 years ago straight after his death and described in the *Nibbana Sutta*. 'They fell down at the Buddha's feet, touched them with their heads, paid homage, stepped back and sat on one side.'5

This literalism is one face of today's Buddha Trail, but next to such a traditionalist approach to pilgrimage others are increasingly being accommodated, with the ease and fluidity that is part of Buddhism and is proving so attractive in particular to Western converts. They find in its ancient wisdom riches that continue to have value in the modern world. In his *Confessions of a Buddhist Atheist*, the British Buddhist teacher Stephen Batchelor, a proponent of what he calls 'secular Buddhism', describes that flexible, open-ended appeal of the Buddhist Trail that each year sees an increase in the number of visitors from Europe and North America. 'You put your body in these places', he writes. 'You hear the same birdsongs. You breathe the same air. You are surrounded by the same trees and foliage that the Buddha may have been surrounded by. And that, somehow, gets you as close as you ever can get physically to the source of the teachings that you are practising in your daily life.'[6]

CHAPTER TEN

SHIKOKU
88 TEMPLES IN THE FOOTSTEPS OF THE GREAT MASTER

'To escape from a morass of depression, to try to find an answer to the problem of how to live, I undertook the [Shikoku] pilgrimage...I made these resolves: to accept whatever happened without anxiety, [and] not to cling to life tenaciously.'

TAKAMURE ITSUE, POET AND HISTORIAN, *MUSUME JUNREIKI* (1979)

The Shikoku pilgrimage has a history stretching back 1,200 years, one for every kilometre of its route round the southern Japanese island of the same name. Much of it is lavishly embroidered with legends about its founder, the monk-scholar Kukai, born in 774, usually known as Kobo Daishi, or Great Teacher, who established the Shingon tradition of Buddhism in Japan. Woven in with the centuries-old stories of the 88-temple walk, though, are contemporary tales that reflect the rapid development since the 1970s of this popular circular pilgrim way.

Initially the modern revival of Shikoku grew out of a movement in Japanese society to reconnect with its own cultural and spiritual heritage. Among the treasures of a 'lost Japan' judged no longer to be sufficiently valued in the country's thriving metropolises, especially among the young, was a rich tradition of finding the sacred in nature on pilgrimage. Some routes where this had been sought in the past were strictly local, but others had been more celebrated nationally, notably the Shikoku path. In the 1960s, with religious observance in Japan on the wane, it had each year seen just 15,000 *henro* – a word that in Japanese means 'remote region' but which, in the context of Shikoku, is preferred for pilgrims to the more standard *junrei*. By the late 1980s, however, that figure had grown to 80,000. Today, an estimated 150,000 circle this, the fourth largest, least developed and greenest, of Japan's many islands, their journeys there made easier by three major bridges that have been built as part of Japan's post-Second World War economic boom, linking it to the bigger island of Honshu across the Inland Sea.[1]

Sprinkled thinly among these growing numbers the faces of *gaijin henro* – foreigner pilgrims – have in the past fifteen years become a more familiar sight. It took until 1921 for the first foreigner to complete the 88-temple circle, the American anthropologist and Japan-expert Frederick Starr. In 2006, just 74 *gaijin henro* were recorded walking it by the local prefecture. A decade later numbers were into the thousands.[2] They have brought with them baggage other than their rucksacks and sturdy walking shoes. Many of those who come from overseas to attempt part, or all of the route or *Henro Michi* (it can, by tradition, be done in stages, year after year, until a full circuit is achieved), are drawn in part by the parallels it offers with their own previous experiences of the Camino in Spain. Both pilgrim trails are, after all, of similar vintage and length. Both cross a diverse, challenging and often breathtakingly beautiful range of landscapes. And popular, too, among such incomers is a modern-day love story, told and retold many times among them as they walk, of a couple who originally met through the Camino, he an American from Texas, she Japanese. They fell for each other, made their home in Japan, but brought a piece of the Camino there with them, establishing their own Camino-style *refugio* in the city of Matsuyama on the Shikoku route. It was simultaneously a bridge between two pilgrimage traditions in different parts of the globe, and an alternative to the long-established Japanese *ryokan* (inns) and *minshuku* (guesthouses) that line the trail, with their futons, rice-straw *tatami* mats and sliding paper-and-bamboo *shoji* screens.

The edges may have been smoothed off in the relaying of this story by *gaijin henro* – some versions say the couple has now turned their backs on the hospitality business – but then tales evolve as part of daily life on pilgrimage trails. While in many other aspects of our modern lives, there is an emphasis placed on being the first, the pioneer, the individual who sees and does things before others and better than them, when it comes to pilgrims, whether they be palmers, *peregrinos* or *henro,* such contemporary obsessions are turned on their head. They draw sustenance and self-insight precisely by not being the first and instead walking in the footsteps of others who have been that way before, in the process retelling and reliving their stories which represent an unbroken human chain through history capable of transcending the here and now.

On Shikoku, with its humid sub-tropical climate next to the Pacific Ocean, the biggest footsteps of all are those of Kobo Daishi. At each of the eighty-eight temples, a statue of him in traditional pilgrim garb, often housed in a small, simple sentry box, greets visitors as they arrive. His words are printed in Japanese on the conical, straw-woven sedge hats that pilgrims wear in imitation of his. And at every single one of these sacred places on the circular pathway there is a legend about Kobo Daishi's association with that particular location that is proudly recounted in a bespoke hymn. Some of the claims made are more firmly grounded in truth than others. Zentsu-ji, Number 75, is said to be his family home (the name honours Kobo Daishi's father) and probably also his birthplace. A giant native camphor tree, which shades the imposing five-storey pagoda, is described as the place where the young Kukai once sat, seeking enlightenment in imitation of the Buddha who, in the sixth century BCE, waited patiently under the Bodhi tree in northern India.

It seems plausible, but then it is just one among several trees at different temples with a similar story to tell. At Number 2, there is a 'Daishi cedar', and at Number 28, another camphor, this time with a carving in its trunk reputedly done by Kobo Daishi with his fingernails in an act of extreme asceticism. The legends are perhaps best seen as traces of the sacred scattered everywhere, like the froth of pink cherry blossom that coats parts of the pilgrim pathway in spring. At Number 3, the Daishi is said to have been in practical mood when he made a spring rise up because locals were short of water. And at Number 6, he is credited with the hot water pouring out that, many believe, can cure illnesses. Numerous *henro* over the centuries, though, have taken such legends as read. Some report receiving their reward for their faith. At various places on the route, displays of discarded braces, crutches and casts bear witness to those who believe they have been cured on the Shikoku Pilgrimage.

Water legends, however, are sufficiently plentiful at other pilgrimage sites around Japan to give pause for thought. Water supply has always been a problem in these islands. It falls in abundance but, when it ran off the mountainous landscape too quickly to be managed, higher powers were invoked. Not just Kobo Daishi, but also the guiding lights of other Buddhist traditions in Japan (Shingon is one of many Buddhist sects followed in some form or other by around 70 per cent of the population), as well as the thousands of nature gods in the pantheon of Shintoism. Japan's home-grown religious tradition predates Buddhism's arrival in these islands and enjoys the nominal attachment of 90 per cent of the population.

Many Japanese combine allegiance to both Shintoism and Buddhism, and the two exist in mutual respect on Shikoku, rooted in their shared veneration of nature. Shinto temples dot the route, and even on occasions share a single site with one of the eighty-eight that recall Kobo Daishi. It hasn't, however, always been quite so harmonious. In the period between the last decades of the nineteenth century and the Second World War, the rise of Japanese nationalism caused a backlash against Shingon, which was labelled as an unwanted import from abroad. Some of its temples on the *Henro Michi* were closed, others vandalized, and even in one case demolished.

Japanese Buddhism, though, can hardly be deemed a recent arrival from overseas. It traces its origins back to the early sixth century CE when the king of Kudara (Paekche), on the southwestern tip of the Korean Peninsula, sent a statue of the Buddha and copies of the great Buddhist texts as part of a diplomatic mission to the Japanese court. It was Kobo Daishi, however, who moulded it into a form that flourished on Japanese soil.

✿

Born on Shikoku, his father a landowner and minor aristocrat distantly related to the once powerful Otomo clan, Kobo Daishi initially followed family expectations. As a young man, he prepared at the university in Nara for a career in government. Political upheavals at court, though, stained the Otomo name and such a future was closed off. It left him free to explore – in the standard neat narrative of his long-ago life – an inner calling that he had been suppressing since childhood. He was drawn to Buddhist scriptures, and set out to explore how he might live what he was reading by meditating and chanting mantras in the mountains of Shikoku.

His decision fully to embrace the priesthood and a life of poverty and service distressed his family but Kobo Daishi refused to bow to their wishes. Later, in the *Sangoshiki*, he described that period, referring to himself in the third person. 'Having no contact with his relatives, he wandered throughout the country like duckweed floating on water or dry glass blown by the wind [and] applied himself diligently to the realization of Buddhism.'³ These wanderings, a pilgrimage in themselves, took him far and wide, including a spell of study in China as part of a Japanese delegation sent by the emperor. Eventually, across the Inland Sea from Shikoku, on the Kii Peninsula, he founded a monastery in 816 on Mount Koya. He was buried there after his death in 835, though some of his devotees continue to believe he is not really dead but instead in eternal meditation in his mausoleum awaiting the arrival of the next Buddha.

Disciples were drawn to him in his lifetime. Alongside his spiritual insights and the simple lifestyle to which he felt himself called, Kobo Daishi was also reputedly a gifted poet, calligrapher and artist. He was even sufficiently versed in engineering to have restored a major reservoir. On occasion, it is said, he would take his band of followers with him over the Inland Sea to Shikoku to walk again through the island's mountains, cedar forests and farming villages as part of the ongoing search for enlightenment. Unlike other branches of Buddhism, Shingon teaches that enlightenment is possible in a single earthly life, though it requires hard and sustained struggle. It does not, as in other sects, require repeated cycles of birth, death and rebirth.

The connection between Kobo Daishi's monastery and his birthplace on Shikoku strengthened in the years that followed his passing. By the tenth century, the temple (now Number 75) at his family home on the north side of the island had been established. That link remains, with some modern pilgrims heading first to the monastery on Mount Koya, a 21-kilometre uphill walk for the hardy, or by train for the softer souls, to prepare for their circuit, before crossing the Inland Sea to Shikoku to start out on the 88-temple route at the nearest port, Tokushima.

The exact evolution of the path that winds from Temple 1 outside Tokushima through all four provinces of Shikoku is nowhere recorded. Legend – there's that word again – would have it that Kobo Daishi himself walked it and mapped it out in its entirety. That belief is best expressed in the oft-told story of Emon Saburo, the first pilgrim to follow the route in Kobo Daishi's lifetime. He was a rich and greedy man, who repeatedly refused when asked to give alms after Kobo Daishi came begging at the gate of his home on the island, which he shared with his eight children. By some accounts he didn't just decline, but broke the begging bowl on one occasion and on another filled it with excrement.

When Kobo Daishi finally moved on, Emon Saburo's children started to die, one after another, day by day. (Some devotees of the Daishi are nervous of this aspect of the story because it shows the Great Teacher as vengeful rather than enlightened.) In despair, their father realized the error of his way, handed over his lands to his tenants, and headed off in pursuit of Kobo Daishi to seek his forgiveness. The route he took is the path of today's pilgrimage. Always a step or two behind, he was forced to beg in order to eat and learnt about humility. Finally, he caught up with Kobo Daishi and was absolved. He died soon afterwards. The site of his grave stands between Temples 12 and 13. The walking stick that he had used as he hurried after Kobo Daishi was planted in the ground next to his burial place and reputedly grew into the cedar that stands there now.

Emon Saburo's story also gives the *Henro Michi* its primary legend – that every pilgrim is never alone. He or she walks the circuit with Kobo Daishi at their side, a connection that finds its clearest expression in two of the distinctive features of the route. Pilgrims carry a walking staff, *kongo-tsue*, imprinted with the words, 'We Two – Pilgrims Together'. And when local people approach them to offer hospitality – still a major feature of the pilgrimage – they will hand over not just one glass of water or bowl of rice, or a cake, but two, one for the pilgrim and one for Kobo Daishi who stands beside, invisible, but in every other way present.

The facts, though, do not always fit with the legend. It is clear that certain sections of Kobo Daishi's route, particularly from what is now Temple 1, Ryozen-ji, in the village of Bando, up through the valley of the Yoshino River to Temple 12, had been a holy route to the mountains long before Kobo Daishi – or his followers – made it his own. The origins of this section of the *Henro Micho* moreover reveal the reverence that mountains have always and still command in Japanese culture in a crowded country where, even today, 70 per cent of all the landmass is designated as national parks, much of it mountainous. In Shinto, as in Shingon Buddhism, mountains are regarded as the home of the souls of ancestors. In other traditions and territories, and at other pilgrimage sites around the globe, mountains are repeatedly taken for the place where heaven and earth meet, where gods descend to rub shoulders with mere mortals (Mount Sinai in the Judeo-Christian canon, Mount Hira in Islam, and Olympus for the Ancient Greeks), but in Japan this is taken one stage further. Ancestors and gods become essentially interchangeable.

Mountains are, therefore, the place to go to feel at one with deceased family members. And so *henro* continue to follow the 88-temple trail up into the mountains carrying in their knapsacks the ashes of their loved ones, or bone fragments, or other mementoes of them, ready to bury or sprinkle them when they reach the heights. Pathways are lined by tall thin gravestones of individual *henro*, usually simply referred to as 'a pilgrim', with no other detail than the date when they died.

That same mountain element is also found on the other national Japanese pilgrim trail to rival Shikoku, the Kumano Kodo. It dates back to the tenth century (younger then than Shikoku) and is found on the Kii peninsula, south of Kyoto, the old imperial capital, and Osaka, as well as of Kobo Daishi's monastery on Mount Koya. A network of pilgrim routes wind their way in the southern end of the peninsula through mountains and forests, past waterfalls and lakes, as they converge on three great shrines.

The history of the Shikoku pilgrimage only gets onto surer historical footing in the seventeenth century. Up to that point, it is believed that it had been known and used mainly by locals, certainly not by the elites from Japan's great cities who would have balked at the trip to primitive Shikoku. Its greatest appeal was to poor island farmers, who would leave their fields to walk sections of it around March and April, in the gap between harvesting their winter wheat and planting the rice seeds in their paddy fields. That period of the year remains its high season. In the second half of the 1600s, however, outsiders started arriving in such numbers that, in 1687 they prompted the appearance of the first *Henro Michi* guidebook, *Shikoku henro michishirube*.

It came in seven slim volumes, printed from woodblocks. The author is believed to have been a local holy man, Yuben Shinnen, who had walked the circuit of temples many times and knew first-hand the challenges the new wave of visitors would face in such rugged terrain. His prescribed route began with Kobo Daishi's family home, Temple 75, and lists another ninety-three. All of today's eighty-eight are there, with the six extras still in service now as *bangai,* or minor shrines.

In the centuries that followed, new traditions and stories continued to be added to what was already an abundant treasury. One favourite saw young men and women from towns on the island, as well as from further afield in Hiroshima, on the other side of the Inland Sea, undertake the *Henro Michi* as a coming-of-age ritual. It counted as proof that they were sufficiently mature for marriage, its physical trials and simple ways seen as perfect preparation for making an adult commitment to another. For the poor among those who took up this challenge, with limited time to spend away from their work, it became a habit to run round rather than walk, so as to complete the whole circuit in the only two weeks they had, quite a feat with 1,200 kilometres to cover. And, as if to demonstrate that, like this pilgrim route, history can also go round in circles, those running would-be bridegrooms and brides of centuries gone by are today replaced by a new generation of present-day young urban Japanese *henro,* who combine exploring their country's past with keeping fit, and tear round the eighty-eight temples in their designer running shoes and lycra, or on expensive mountain bikes.

❁

All faiths have their significant numbers – three, seven, ten, twelve, forty being the most common and shared across denominational boundaries. Buddhism is no exception. It teaches of three realms or worlds – of desire, of form, or without form – and four noble truths, eight auspicious symbols of the Buddha, and eighty-eight passions or defilements that humankind passes from generation to generation. Did this final calibration play any part in the designation of eighty-eight temples on Shikoku, rather than the ninety-four that Yuben Shinnen listed in the original guidebook?

Again the history is hazy, but symbols remain integral to the *Henro Michi*, especially to the estimated 5,000 pilgrims who walk it, as opposed to the much larger number who hop on and off buses and coaches or take short cuts on their travels round it, often experiencing only a 'greatest hits' selection of the temples. White, for example, is the Japanese colour of death, the equivalent of black in the West. The majority of *henro* tackling the trail in earnest still wear traditional white, in their hip-length jackets or *hakui*, and (less often) in the accompanying trousers, the combination reflecting the belief that to attempt the circuit, as a whole or in parts in successive years, is to risk death. Enlightenment on earth, Kobo Daishi insisted, was possible but not easily attained. With three mountain ranges, climbing up to 1,000 metres at Temple 66, the highest spot on the route, not to mention the endless staircases cut into steep slopes to reach many of the temples, and more recently the necessity of dodging the incessant traffic on busy roads that have encroached on the old pilgrim route in more popular parts of the island, the *Henro Michi* is no extended stroll in the park.

The symbolism stretches further to other pilgrim accoutrements. As well as the walking staff – as already mentioned, representing the presence of Kobo Daishi at each pilgrim's side – there is the brass bell that hangs from many a serious pilgrim's belt. They ring it, when arriving at a temple, as another reminder of human impermanence, its sound fading quickly as it is absorbed by nature.

Then there is a 108-bead rosary or *nenju*, plus the *nokyocho* – the pilgrim passport in which stamps from each temple can be gathered – and a pack of *osamefuda*, or name slips, imprinted with the Daishi's profile, on which pilgrims write invocations to the gods for health and happiness as well as their name and address, and leave at the temples they visit. These papers are gathered at the end of each day and eventually burned in batches, the prayers on them, it is believed, ascending in tendrils of smoke to the temple's presiding deity for their attention. Most *henro* use white slips, but for that doughty few who have made the circuit five or six times, they are green, then red for seven to twenty-four completed circles, silver for twenty-five to forty-nine, and gold for anyone who has done more.

Symbolism turns into measurement, too, with the eighty-eight stopping places on the route divided into four distinct stages. Each represents one of the four stages on the path to enlightenment: Temples 1 to 23 are awakening; 24 to 39 austerity and discipline; 40 to 65 attaining enlightenment; and 66 to 88 entering Nibbana/ Nirvana (or heaven). One of the quirks of Buddhism, though, is that it manages to be both carefully organized and portioned out, as well as flexible enough to accommodate each pilgrim as an individual. Many pilgrims do not follow the prescribed order of the eighty-eight temples, and instead start midway through. Others do the whole thing back to front. In both cases, they are rewarded with encouragement. The twentieth-century Japanese feminist poet and historian Takamure Itsue, quoted at the start of this chapter, completed a circuit in 1918. 'Doing it in reverse,' she reported, 'the hills are steeper and so it is considered more difficult and more meritorious.'

What is unchanging, and unchangeable, is the circular shape of the route. Unlike other more linear pilgrimage paths included in this book, circles can have no beginning and no ending. They therefore accommodate the aspiration to go all the way round, with a journey's end when the original destination is reached again, but there is also the added symbolism of having closed the circle. Arguably it better expresses the ambition that it is the journey, rather than the destination, which lies at the heart of pilgrimage. It also opens the possibility to going round again as a version of the seamless, never-ending journey towards enlightenment.

In such a scheme, the individual characteristics of each temple become less important. Yet the eighty-eight on the *Henro Michi* are by no means uniform. Koon-ji, Number 61, for example, stands alone by having a modern brutalist concrete main hall, where the rest have time-honoured wooden structures. Some temples are large complexes, others small cubby holes, perching on a ledge, high up a mountain, with panoramic views. There is, however, a degree of uniformity. They all have their own two-storey gate-house, or *sanmon,* often with a flaring tiled roof that in some cases reaches out and up in dolphin shapes that flip their tails in greeting. Inside the compound, all will provide a stone ablution basin for the arriving pilgrims to undergo a symbolic purification, with long bamboo-handled ladles. There is the large brass bell, or *bonsho,* hanging with a heavy piece of timber that can be swung to make it ring out, and announce new arrivals to the temple deity and the Daishi.

Unlike some of the grand temples in Japan's major cities, the eighty-eight on Shikoku have a lived-in, sometimes even scruffy feel. They are places where pilgrims can participate in worship, rather than museums where they stand and watch. At the entrance to the main hall or *hondo,* there are candles to light, incense sticks to burn, and a bow to be made. The resident priest – who may be willing to offer pilgrims hospitality at the end of the day in the temple's outbuildings – could be carrying out rituals, accompanied by chanting, bells and drums. Or, in quieter times, individual *henro* are left alone to make their own prayers.

Some rituals are dramatic, especially those that revolve around fire – which, among other things in Buddhism, symbolizes the self. The *hiwatari,* where priests and sometimes willing pilgrims walk barefoot on hot coals, is one crowd-pleasing ritual of Shingon Buddhists. But, on Shikoku, the clerics do not dominate. This is an island whose legend is one of wandering holy men, not priests leading from the front.

Present-day pilgrims – including that increasing number of them who are foreigners – are more likely to have encounters with local people on the route than with priests. When they do, thanks to the tradition of *settai* that still operates – where visitors to the island must be shown hospitality – food or drink or sometimes lodging are proffered with the words, '*O henro san*' ('Dear Mr/Mrs Pilgrim'), the belief behind it that such generosity pleases Kobo Daishi. And in that moment, in the spirit of pilgrimage, two worlds, ancient and modern, come face to face.

CHAPTER 11

NORTH AMERICA
OPTIMISTIC HIKING

✳

'So they lefte [that] goodly & pleasante citie, which had been ther resting place, nere 12 years; but they knew they were pilgrimes, & looked not much on these things; but lift up their eyes to ye heavens, their dearest cuntrie, and quieted their spirits.'

WILLIAM BRADFORD, *OF PLIMOTH PLANTATION* (1651)[1]

Pilgrimage has usually been regarded as a collective endeavour, either directly as part of an organized group, or undertaken by an individual following a pilgrim trail and interacting with others doing the same thing. Mildred Norman did something rather different. In the pioneer spirit of her native United States, the same spirit that had seen the Pilgrim Fathers, as they became known, escape religious persecution in Anglican England for their Puritan views by crossing the Atlantic on the *Mayflower* to establish Plymouth Colony in Massachusetts in 1620, Norman set off alone in her mid-forties to cross North America. She did it six times in all between 1952 and her death in 1981, covering in the process more than 40,000 kilometres (after a certain point she said that she stopped counting). She was always dressed in a trademark blue tunic that announced her mission in the big, bold, unmissable and unambiguous hand-stitched letters as 'Peace Pilgrim'. 'I shall remain a wanderer,' she insisted to those she met when she walked through their towns, 'until mankind has learned the ways of peace'.[2]

The Pilgrim Fathers – a name that they did not use of themselves, but under which they continue to exert a hold on the American imagination – were not fans of traditional pilgrimage. Their theology was on the other end of the religious spectrum from Catholicism. As thorough-going Protestants growing up in post-Reformation England, looking out on still largely Catholic Europe, they would have seen pilgrimage as a kind of worship of false idols, since it tried to give a physical form and setting to faith that had to be essentially immaterial. It was no doubt an objection that they carried with them to their New World and explains in some measure why it has long shaped America's lack of widespread enthusiasm on home soil for pilgrimage. But the Pilgrim Fathers might still have managed a sneaking regard for Mildred Norman and her determination, by using pilgrimage, to express views that were regarded as heretical in the political, cultural and spiritual changing times, in her case Cold War America of the 1950s and 1960s.

Initially those who encountered Peace Pilgrim (she didn't like the definite article to be attached) regarded her as an eccentric. In the land of the automobile, here was someone who preferred to rely on tennis shoes to propel herself (she claimed to get at least 2,500 kilometres wear out of each pair). She referred to herself as an 'optimistic hiker', which meant in practice that she carried no great rucksack, or even a sleeping mat, instead relying on the kindness and charity of the strangers she encountered. It was also a throwback to the lifestyle of the original mendicant orders in Christianity, such as the Franciscans and Dominicans.

In twelfth- and thirteenth-century Europe their founders reacted to the rise of a money-based economy by taking to the road unencumbered by possessions so as more effectively to serve those in need around them. Like them, Norman lived on the generosity of others. When it failed to materialize – she would never produce a begging bowl – she would sleep in bus stations or cornfields at the side of the highway.

Her single-mindedness and her dedication to making her life a counterpoint to the values of the modern world gradually drew more and more attention to her pilgrim message of peace. So much so that, by the time of her death, a formal nomination had been made on her behalf to the organizing committee of the Nobel Peace Prize. Originally a poultry farmer's daughter from New Jersey, her seamless thirty-year pilgrimage had begun familiarly enough in troubled times after the failure of her marriage. Seeking space to reflect on life's ups and downs, she set out in 1952 on foot unaccompanied, unsupported and carrying with her little more than the comb, folding toothbrush and pen that fitted in her pockets, to walk the 3,500 kilometre-long Appalachian Trail that runs from New England down to Georgia in the eastern United States. Somewhere along the way, she experienced a vision that was to shape the rest of her life and give birth to her pilgrim mission. It was revealed to her, she wrote in her memoir, that this was, 'the proper time for a pilgrim to step forth. The war in Korea was raging and the McCarthy era was at its height … There was a great fear at that time and it was safest to be apathetic. Yes, it was most certainly a time for a pilgrim to step forward, because a pilgrim's job is to rouse people from apathy and make them think.'[3]

That is what this smiling, grey-haired woman did. Asked by an admirer why she didn't want to give her birth name or details of her earlier life, she replied: 'I would much rather they remember the important things instead of the very unimportant thing.[4] There may have been another reason. The FBI, keen at the time on rooting out communists, had started to ask questions about her and she wanted to protect her family. By living as a nameless perpetual pilgrim in utter simplicity and spiritual trust, she made an impact. Her willingness to engage saw her interviewed by newspapers and local radio stations along the routes she trod. Those who met her and gave her a place to sleep and food to eat would sometimes facilitate impromptu local meetings where others could gather to listen to what she had to say of her travels and the impetus behind them. She would talk about peace – between nations, between individuals, and inside each individual – as well as her own 'on foot and on faith' spirituality. At the end, she would hand out the small leaflets she carried with her.

Peace Pilgrim offered from her own experience a powerful modern-day endorsement of the time-honoured value of pilgrimage to transport individuals to a vantage point from where the world looked very different.

> *I was out walking in the early morning. All of a sudden I felt very uplifted, more uplifted than I had ever been. I remember I knew timelessness and spacelessness and lightness. I did not seem to be walking on the earth. There were no people, or even animals around, but every flower, every bush, every tree seemed to wear a halo. There was a light emanation around everything and flecks of gold fell like slanted rain through the air ... The most important part was not the phenomena: the important part of it was the realization of the oneness of all creation.*[5]

Her death at the age of 72 – or her 'glorious transition' as she referred to it as she got older – did little to stem the tide of interest in her.

In the years since, over 1.5 million copies of her short booklet, *Steps Toward Inner Peace,* have been printed and distributed in English by Friends of Peace Pilgrim, the organization set up in her memory. It has been translated into thirty-one languages. As a patron saint of the modern pilgrim, she is hard to better.

✿

While North America has a scattering of pilgrimage destinations, not least among them the Pilgrim Monument in Massachusetts to those early Puritan settlers, it is short on actual historical pilgrimage routes to rival those found on other continents. The being-in-a-sacred-place aspect of pilgrimage is reasonably served, but those wanting to prepare physically and spiritually by following a well-trodden path to such spots are not. It may explain why Peace Pilgrim's wanderings over the decades saw her crisscrossing the United States (including Alaska and Hawaii), Mexico and Canada, apparently at random. There were no established pilgrim trails for her to follow.

Her first 'official' pilgrimage, though, reveals a more complex story of pilgrimage in North America. It took place in 1953, after she had been shown the pattern of the rest of her life on the Appalachian Trail. This time Peace Pilgrim started out at the annual 'Rose Parade' in Pasadena in California, where she walked among the crowds handing out leaflets about her peace mission, and then set off for Washington, DC, a trek that was to take her eleven months. If there is no authorized route, much less a pilgrim path in the United States, her ambition of going coast to coast certainly resonated in the nation's psyche – for historical, geographical and civic reasons, if not precisely spiritual ones. That push ever westwards after the first settlers had followed the Pilgrim Fathers' example and established colonies on the east coast, that drive to explore and expand that conquered every physical obstacle encountered in this vast landscape, including its indigenous inhabitants, was undertaken on foot, on horseback, in wagon trains or on the newly constructed railroads that eventually bridged and brought together the continent. It is a key and revered part of the foundation story of America. And then there was, and to an extent remains, a very particular reverence among Americans around making a visit to the federal capital, Washington, DC. Seeing Washington became for many Americans something akin to a civic pilgrimage to a constitutionally, and nationally, sacred shrine.

Seen in this context, the ultimate destination of the pilgrimage is the National Mall, that expanse of green parkland in the very heart of Washington that contains memorials to two of America's most revered presidents, Abraham Lincoln and George Washington, as well as the seat of government on Capitol Hill, the National Museum of American History, the National Museum of African American History and Culture, and monuments to those who have sacrificed their lives in defence of America's liberty in overseas wars in Europe, Korea and Vietnam. Landscape, history, identity, allegiance and self-belief are seamlessly interwoven in this corridor that attracts twenty-four million visitors annually. An insight into the degree of quasi-religious reverence with which it continues to be regarded by Americans came in 2013 when *National Geographic Magazine*, marking the fiftieth anniversary of the March on Washington for Jobs and Freedom, headed by Martin Luther King, Jr., named the demonstration its 'top historic pilgrimage'.

The use of the p-word might, of course, be justified by the religious overtones to an event that culminated in 250,000 people gathering on the National Mall on 28 August 1963. Pastors, priests and rabbis were prominent among those who stood on the steps

15 Sadhus or holy men during Kumbh Mela,
Prayag, India.

16 Kumbh Mela, Prayag, India.

17 Monks praying in front of the Bodhi Tree where
the Buddha experienced enlightenment, Bodh Gaya, India.

18 The capital of the Ashokean pillar at Sarnath, India, 3rd century BCE.

19 *Henro*, or a Japanese Buddhist pilgrim, at Tokushima on
Shikoku island, dressed in the traditional pilgrim costume
of a white jacket and carrying a wooden staff.

20 Kobo Daishi (Kukai) (774–835), founder of the Shikoku pilgrirmage, depicted in a 14th-century scroll.

July, 1847.   ROUTE OF THE MORMON PIONE

21 A map produced in 1897 to commemorate the fiftieth anniversary of the journey of the Mormon pioneers from Nauvoo to Great Salt Lake. It shows the daily progress along the route.

22 Mormon pageant at Hill Cumorah, New York.

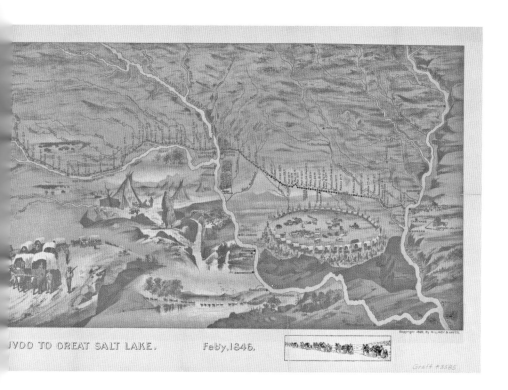

JVOO TO GREAT SALT LAKE.   Feb'y,1846.

23 Martin Luther King, Jr., at the March on Washington for Jobs and Freedom, Washington, DC, 28 August 1963. It was here that he made his famous 'I Have a Dream' speech.

24 Front gate of the sanctuary at Chimayo, New Mexico, USA.

25 The 15th-century Inca citadel of Machu Picchu, Peru.

of the Lincoln Memorial. And in the Reverend Martin Luther King, Jr.'s 'I Have a Dream' speech, delivered that day, there was an abundance of biblical imagery and imperatives to be found in his appeal for civic and economic equality. Yet what also made a march and rally into a pilgrimage, at least for *National Geographic*, was the sacred significance of the place where the crowd had stood that day to hear Dr King's words.

In the same way, other routes the Peace Pilgrim travelled in her mission shed light on a distinctively North American approach to pilgrimage. Her original inspiration to be a pilgrim, as John Bunyan might have put it, came to her while on the Appalachian Trail, one of the series of designated national pathways that stretch across vast areas of mountains, forests, deserts and plains. These are places where what is sometimes called 'the religion of the wild' can be experienced full throttle, alongside a daunting physical challenge. Moreover, the confluence between some of these national trails and sites sacred to indigenous American peoples, with their beliefs in the physical manifestation of a Great Spirit in and through the landscape, adds an element of getting in touch with the 'other' to walking them. It is the same thing Celtic monks in the sixth century sought as they headed to the west coast of Wales.

Yet the word pilgrimage is rarely publicly or officially associated with the national, government-funded trails in a country that formally separates Church and State. Where it is heard more frequently in North America is in relation to specific religious destinations. Often these are places that were originally developed as part of an enduring emotional and spiritual connection with their 'home' countries by the wave after wave of immigrants, especially from Catholic Europe, or south of the border with Mexico, who have come seeking a new life in the United States and Canada. Though the first arrivals in the US were from Puritan and Protestant backgrounds, there were already French Catholic settlers in Canada when the Pilgrim Fathers reached land. And, at 22 per cent of the population, Catholics now make up the single largest religious group in the United States, with nearly half of all Americans reporting some connection to Catholicism. Over the border in Canada, around 35 per cent are Catholic. And so, inevitably, traditional devotions to the Virgin Mary – and to what is believed to be her ability to work miracles – have been replicated in both countries.

At Attleboro in Massachusetts, there is the National Shrine of Our Lady of La Salette, effectively a homage to the shrine in the French Alps that celebrates the Vatican-approved reports of the Virgin Mary appearing to young children there in 1846. Likewise, there is the Saint Laurent Shrine in rural Saskatchewan, also known in Canada as its very own Our Lady of Lourdes. From the late 1870s onwards, there were reports at Saint Laurent of miraculous cures of those who were anointed with water that flowed from a spring on the hillside above this small Catholic church into a specially constructed grotto. Since 1905 there have been annual pilgrimages throughout the summer season with all the features of the European Marian tradition described in Chapter Six.

Yet there is no corresponding pilgrim route leading to these, or to the host of other similar Catholic shrines that imitate the well-trodden paths to Rome, Walsingham or Santiago de Compostela. The cause for the omission may be partly one of timing. In the medieval period, the vast majority of European pilgrims wanting to visit holy places had no choice but to walk and so pathways were created. By the time the North American shrines arose, there were railways and later cars and coaches to carry them there, at much greater speed, with no need for wayside resting places and *refugios*. And then, in the United States in particular, there was long a sense within the Catholic community of needing to keep a low profile in a nation that for centuries proudly saw itself as primarily WASP (white, Anglo-Saxon and Protestant), drawing on strands of Christianity that had at the Reformation rejected the flamboyant manifestations, miracles and Mariology of Rome. It might tolerate their churches and communities, these American Catholics decided, but not their pilgrimage trails laying claim to corridors through the countryside. Such perceptions were slow to change. John F. Kennedy, after all, was in 1960 the first Catholic to be elected as President of the United States and during his campaign faced a barrage of anti-Catholic prejudice.

Quite how far that has disappeared in the twenty-first century can be seen by a rash of recent efforts to create pilgrim trails, often inspired by Americans who – like Martin Sheen's character in *The Way* – have experienced the Camino in Spain, and been moved to replicate it on their own doorstep once home. In a 2016 survey of visitors compiled by the Pilgrims' Office in Santiago de Compostela, Americans made up the fourth largest national group on the Camino that year (after Spaniards, Italians and Germans).

One such scheme, still in its infancy, is the 185-kilometre pilgrimage trail promoted as the Camino del Norte at Chimayo in the southwestern state of New Mexico. It is an expansion of an existing local Easter pilgrimage tradition at the sanctuary at Chimayo, where for decades walkers, some carrying life-size replicas of Jesus' cross on Calvary, others parking their cars alongside the highway north from Santa Fe and covering the last few kilometres on foot, arrive at the early nineteenth-century rough-hewn adobe church at Chimayo (declared a National Historical Landmark by the American authorities as far back as 1970).

'Like much of northern New Mexico,' wrote the award-winning American social and cultural historian Rebecca Solnit, who visited Chimayo for her 2001 study of walking, *Wanderlust*, 'the town exudes a sense of ancientness that sets it apart from the rest of the forgetful United States ... Walking cross-country let us be in that nonbeliever's paradise, nature, before we arrived at this most traditional of religious destinations.'[6]

Built by local landowner Don Bernardo Abeyta around 1810 on the site of a spring regarded as sacred by local Tewa Indians, the small, sturdy Chimayo sanctuary was an offshoot of another shrine, the 'Black' Christ of Esquipulas in Guatemala. Don Bernardo's church co-opted Esquipulas's claims as a place of healing. In a small, unpaved chapel, a hole in the floor contains moist, crumbly mud that pilgrims scoop up as 'holy dirt'. It is a curious variation on the holy well. At an earlier date the mud was added to water and drunk as a curative brew. Today it is rubbed on the body in the belief that it can bring about miraculous remission from ailments. As if to prove the point, in the sanctuary, walls once more are lined with discarded crutches and plaster casts.

The extended Camino version of this tradition seeks better to marry those elements of eternal nature and traditional religion that Solnit identified in a pilgrimage trail that will operate for more than a few days a year. Taking seven to ten days to complete, the new trail carries 'optimistic hikers' from San Luis in Colorado to Chimayo via forest trails, and sparsely populated, desert-like areas of sagebrush flats, and mountains.

At the other end of the continent, in the Canadian province of Quebec, another Camino-inspired pilgrimage route has been established by Canadian artist Sylvie Cimon, following her return home from Spain. The Sentier Notre-Dame Kapatakan – which takes ten days to walk – is known as 'Little Compostela' and was created in the first decade of the twenty-first century with financial support from the Canadian government. Located north of Quebec City, it carves out a 215-kilometre pathway through mountains and along the shore of fjords between two long-established local pilgrimage destinations that belong to an earlier age of faith. The starting point is a dramatic 9-metre-tall, late nineteenth-century wood-and-lead statue of Our Lady of Sagueney that overlooks a tributary of the Saint Lawrence. It was put up in thanks by a man, caught on breaking ice on the river, who would in all normal circumstances have drowned, but who attributed his survival to the intervention of the Virgin Mary. And the trail ends at the Hermitage of Saint Antoine, a Capuchin retreat centre in the Lac-Saint-Jean area that, since the early decades of the twentieth century, has been a popular place of pilgrimage for French-speaking local Catholics seeking to get closer to God through immersion in nature.

❁

Peace Pilgrim walked not just for herself, and her spiritual well-being, but also to evangelize in the cause of peace – by her example, by her sheer stamina, and by her words. Hers was a gentle approach to evangelizing, certainly no hard sell, but effective nonetheless as her continuing reputation demonstrates. A similar evangelistic take on pilgrimage can be seen in the activities of the Church of Jesus Christ of Latter-day Saints, better known as the Mormons. With fifteen million members around the world, it is America's largest home-grown denomination. For the past eight decades, it has promoted a pilgrimage to a place known to Mormons as Hill Cumorah, near the small town of Palmyra, southeast of Rochester in New York State.

The 243-acre site at Hill Cumorah is the birthplace of the Mormon Church. In 1823, it is taught, their founder, Joseph Smith, who lived here on a farm with his devoutly Christian family, was visited by an angel who identified himself by the name Moroni.

As part of a series of revelations to 18-year-old Smith, the angel directed him to a stash of gold tablets buried in a stone box in the side of a small hill nearby. For four years, Smith could see but not touch the tablets. When the angel finally gave him permission to unearth them, he also endowed him with the power to translate what was written on them. The account Smith read was of a lost Judeo-Christian civilization, native to North America, which had been wiped out by internecine battles. In 1830, he published it as *The Book of Mormon*, explaining in an introduction that, once he had completed his translation, the angel took back the plates.

In the text, there is mention of a place sacred to the lost civilization of the Nephites, known as Cumorah. Many Mormons believe that place is their pilgrimage site and so have named it Hill Cumorah. In the 1920s, the expanding Church of Jesus Christ of Latter-day Saints purchased the land around Smith's old home so as to allow pilgrims access to the sacred grove where the golden tablets are said to have been buried. In 1935, it was decided to introduce something more evangelistic. The annual Hill Cumorah Pageant began, attracting pilgrims to Palmyra around 24 July, a date designated in the Mormon calendar as Pioneer Day, marking the arrival in 1847 of a wagon train of Mormons into Salt Lake City, to this day the headquarters of their Church.

Initially the pageant was a modest enough affair, the stage lit by the headlights of parked cars for a re-enactment of the events described in *The Book of Mormon* in the form of a play, known from 1937 as *America's Witness for Christ*. It quickly drew a crowd of thousands of Mormon pilgrims from around the United States, and often from overseas. It is estimated that as many as five million people had seen the play by the time the Church decided to make the 2021 production the final Cumorah Pageant. Many of them would have been Mormons, gathered there on pilgrimage, but many too were those who came along out of curiosity to find out more about a Church that had enjoyed a controversial reputation in the United States from its earliest days, not least for its practice of polygamy. By opening the doors of the pageant to all-comers free-of-charge, the Church sought to give a more positive public account of itself. That aim proved successful, with plenty of those who came along going on to become members. Pilgrimage was a tool of evangelization.

Those being evangelized, though, were not only the non-Mormons in an annual audience that grew to 25,000. It was also Mormons themselves, for the cast of the play, 700-strong, as well as the production crew, was made up almost entirely of pilgrims. Participation front and backstage became a key part of the pilgrimage experience. As soon as they arrived, whole families of Mormons, young and old alike, took part in vast open auditions held over a single day. Those who were unsuccessful were encouraged to come back and try again the following year, while the chosen many would throw themselves into rehearsals and then performances over a seven-day period, emerging knowing the holy book of their faith better than ever before.

If it sounds a curious undertaking on first hearing – and the pageant was parodied in opening scenes of the highly successful 2011 musical *The Book of Mormon* – such an approach is not without precedent. Its most obvious roots are in a mid-nineteenth- to early twentieth-century American predilection for staging local and regional public carnivals and pageants that celebrated the area. Going further back, there are echoes too of the miracle, passion and mystery plays that were the great public spectacles of medieval Europe. For some Mormons, especially those from families of modest means, the pilgrimage to Palmyra was a crowning once-in-a-lifetime experience (especially if they ended up on stage), as

Mecca is for Moslems or Kumbh for Hindus. There were also other pageants the Church organized, but Hill Cumorah stood head and shoulders above the rest because of the historical ground on which it was staged.

In 2018, the Mormon authorities decided to end the tradition of the pageant – though the visitor centre at the site, and the sacred grove, will remain open after 2021. Ideas of pilgrimage and evangelization – though still linked – were changing, they argued, with the emphasis shifting towards pilgrimage being seen as travelling, often to foreign countries, to evangelize by different means in the name of the Church rather than concentrating so much energy and resources on a single site in New York State. 'Local celebrations of culture and history may be appropriate,' the official announcement read. 'Larger productions, such as pageants, are discouraged.'

Yet as one door closed on long-held notions of pilgrimage in the Church of Jesus Christ of Latter-day Saints, another was starting to open – or, more accurately re-open. For the Mormons are inextricably linked with what can justifiably claim to be America's only major religious pilgrimage route. In 1978, President Jimmy Carter added five new 'National Historic Trails' to the existing portfolio of 'National Scenic Trails' (including the Appalachian one) that had been run by the National Park Service since 1968. Among them was the Mormon Pioneer National Historic Trail, a 2,000-kilometre route from Illinois via Iowa, Nebraska and Wyoming to Salt Lake City in Utah.

The history it tells is of the troubled early days of the Church that Joseph Smith had founded. After attracting many thousands of converts following the publication of *The Book of Mormon*, Smith and his followers saw their efforts to establish a base in one settled place frustrated by a combination of internal disputes and external hostility. By 1844, they had moved progressively further westwards to escape their detractors and ended up in the frontier town of Nauvoo, on a bend of the Mississippi in Illinois. Even there they could not find the religious freedom that they sought. Another confrontation landed Smith behind bars, where he was murdered, aged 38, when an angry mob stormed the jailhouse.

A battle then ensued among his followers over the succession, settled in 1846 when Brigham Young emerged. The Mormons' position in Nauvoo was untenable, he decided, and so he led around 14,000 Mormons westwards in search of the great salt-lake valley of which he had heard reports. It was an isolated place, he had been told, and hence somewhere he hoped his fledgling church could go about its business undisturbed. The route the Mormons took is the basis of today's Mormon Pioneer National Historic Trail. They may not have been the first to tread it down. Others had gone that way before, following existing indigenous pathways as part of a wider movement of people westwards to make their fortune. What ended up forging the association that has endured ever after between the Mormons and this route, however, was the extremes of suffering they faced on it, and the unbreakable spirit they showed on their pilgrimage in finally making it to their promised Zion.

The plan had been to plant small settlements of Mormons along the trail, leaving members of the party behind, so that those who followed would have places to stop and a warm welcome from fellow believers. Young and 143 others went on ahead of the main group, wintering in Nebraska in 1846, surviving cold, cholera and a series of back-breaking climbs, finally to arrive at the ridge on Big Mountain, part of the Wasatch range, where they saw the fabled salt valley spread out before them. 'This is the place', Young is reputed to have said at that moment. 'Drive on.' His words feature on a plaque that marks the spot on the modern trail.

Their westerly exodus is painted in the annals of the Church as the equivalent of a biblical epic, in which Brigham Young is cast as the 'Mormon Moses'. The legend of those pioneers who survived the hardship continues to be reflected in the honour societies of Mormons – the Sons and Daughters of the Utah Pioneers. And where the first group had blazed the trail, others quickly followed, encouraged by the Perpetual Emigration Fund the Mormons set up in 1850 to enable them to charter ships to carry poor European migrants across the Atlantic, and once landed to make their way to Utah. Over the next two decades another 80,000 arrived, many enduring times on the route as hellish as those that afflicted the original pioneers, with consumption rife and children's lives lost, as they noted down in mournful entries to the diaries they kept.

In 1869, however, the transcontinental railroad reached Utah and Union Pacific trains could now carry new arrivals to Salt Lake City. So the trail fell into disuse, with most traces of it eventually wiped off the map. It was only in the 1930s, to mark the centenary of the publication of *The Book of Mormon* that a movement began to locate and save as much of it as could be salvaged. The best-preserved sections of the Mormon Pioneer National Trail are nowadays on the final stage, closest to Salt Lake City. Walkers and pilgrims can tackle it in on foot and by car. Numbers remain relatively small. With so many breaks, where the old trail disappears underneath private land, it remains a work in progress. As do efforts to emphasize not only the physical endurance of those pioneers who used it in the middle of the nineteenth century, but also their pilgrim intent.

Maps and guidebooks have been produced by a dedicated band of enthusiasts but, where traces of its Mormon past can be glimpsed, they do not always create the best impression of the Church. In Echo Canyon, the remains of fortifications can be seen that were built by Brigham Young in 1857 as he prepared to resist an attempt by President James Buchanan to assert federal control over Mormon Utah. Battle may never have been joined, but they are reminders of the awkward position the Mormons have long held in America, and to some extent still do. In 2012, the Republican presidential candidate, Mitt Romney, faced intense scrutiny over whether his religious affiliation to the Church of Jesus Christ of Latter-day Saints could or should disqualify him to be head of state.

It may be one of the reasons why the Mormon Pioneer Trail is struggling to achieve the sort of revival that similar routes in France, Germany, Italy, Wales and Spain are experiencing. In many ways Europe is now post-Christian, and the claims of institutional religion to authority over the lives of populations have been consigned to history. Walking a route where the faithful once walked therefore carries with it little negative baggage (allowing space for the more positive things about faith to emerge). However, the enduring reputation of the Church of Jesus Christ of Latter-day Saints makes anything labelled Mormon likely to be treated with a certain caution. That rather inhibits the open-hearted, open-minded pilgrim embrace found on the Camino. Time will tell if the Mormon Pioneer Trail evolves to replicate those attributes and achieve the Camino's wide resonance.

CHAPTER 12

MACHU PICCHU
POWER PLACES

※

*'In the nineteenth century, it was London, Paris, Rome,
and Greece. Today it's a global buffet: a safari in Africa,
the Great Wall of China, the Taj Mahal, Machu Picchu,
and the Carnival, in Brazil.'*

PAUL THEROUX[1]

'We rounded the promontory and were confronted by an unexpected sight,' writes the Yale University historian and swashbuck-
ling explorer Hiram Bingham of the moment, on the morning of 24
July 1911, when he followed a local guide, 11-year-old Pablito Alvarez,
through a rainforest, up a mountain and stumbled into the 'lost'
Inca citadel that he named Machu Picchu after the cloud-fringed
crag in whose shadow it stood. Before his eyes, he recalled, was
spread out 'a great flight of beautifully constructed stone-faced
terraces, perhaps a hundred of them, each hundreds of feet long
and ten feet high [and] the walls of ruined houses built of the finest
quality Inca stone work … partly covered with trees and moss, the
growth of centuries … The sight held me spellbound … It seemed
like an unbelievable dream. What could this place be?'[2]

What was laid out before him in such an unlikely location was sufficient to make his head spin, though the high altitude, 2,500 metres up in the Peruvian Andes, where the air is thin, may have played a part. The same sensation is now experienced every day by the 5,000 visitors who hike up in the high season between May and August to Machu Picchu (their number capped to prevent further damage to what is now a UNESCO World Heritage Site). Yet their trailblazer, Professor Bingham, his publicity picture in wide-brimmed hat, neckerchief and khaki 'jungle' clothes said to have been the inspiration for Hollywood's favourite adventurer, Indiana Jones, may have allowed a note of hyperbole to creep into his breathless account. For this was, it turned out decades later, not the lost Inca city of Vilcabamba, the final stronghold of the last emperor, Mancho Inca, for which Bingham had been searching. That was subsequently unearthed in 1964 on a site he had visited prior to Machu Picchu, but dismissed.

And neither had Machu Picchu – 'old peak' in the local Quechua language of the Andean highlands – ever really been lost. Though long deserted, it had certainly remained hidden from the Spanish conquistadors who came in the sixteenth century (there are no accounts of anything resembling Machu Picchu in any of the much-studied chronicles of the Spanish invasion and occupation). Locals, however, always knew it was up there, invisible from below in its bird's nest perch on a narrow saddle of land between two peaks and protected from below by the Urubamba River that coils round its base like a snake. They are thought to have taken other adventurers up there in the late nineteenth century, but these guests lacked Bingham's knack for turning his discovery into international headlines via a spread in *National Geographic Magazine*. When young Pablito led Bingham up there, some of the local farmers were even using parts of the original, intricate, stone-built terraces that tame the mountainside around the Inca citadel to grow potatoes, corn and sugar cane.

Yet there was and remains an undeniable air of mystery around Machu Picchu that draws increasing numbers of visitors – close on 1.6 million in 2018, up from just 150,000 in 1980. Because so much about this implausible site is so unclear, those who come, whether historians, archaeologists, tourists or pilgrims, can super-impose their own ideas and beliefs onto it, just as Bingham did when he (re)discovered it. Quite what Machu Picchu once was, or had been when it was built to such exacting standards in the fifteenth century, and then for no discernable reason abandoned 100 years later, remains the subject of much speculation and little consensus. Even its name is in doubt. Bingham may have chosen to call it Machu Picchu but some of the many who have written extensively on the subject since claim it was known to its Inca creators as Yllampu, Quechua for 'the dwelling place of the gods'.[3]

That connection with the gods, with the divine and the world of spirits, whether up in the skies, in nature, or even in the earth in what is one of the planet's 'thin' places seemingly designed to direct our gaze to the heavens, has come to give Machu Picchu a particular appeal for those modern-day spiritual seekers, popularly known as New Agers. They head in numbers along the Inca Trail constructed 500 years ago across the Andes. Sometimes they are accompanied as 'spirit guides' by local shamans who are found in greater than usual density in the area, part of a network of small but vibrant communities with their own rituals and names like Children of the Sun – Inti Churincura – drawing inspiration from the Inca worship of a sun god. And once they arrive at Machu Picchu, their efforts to perform their particular ceremonies can cause problems for the authorities who oversee the site. Some shamans – to whom are attributed special powers to enter the world of the spirits – advise that the Intihuatana Stone, arguably Machu Picchu's most popular and most mysterious attraction, will bring enlightenment if touched with the forehead. Yet that risks wearing it away, archaeologists have counselled, and so the historical and the spiritual pull in opposite directions, with a guard posted by the stone to keep it safe during opening hours. The same remedy was adopted when some visitors, seeking better to absorb the earth's energies at what they believed to be a sacred spot, started to take off their clothes to feel the full force.

The conviction that Machu Picchu has a peculiar power to unlock and afford access to an ancient, lost religion runs deep. It has been part of its DNA since Bingham published his first speculations about the site. He posited that Machu Picchu was the mythical Tamba Tocco, a kind of Garden of Eden in Inca mythology that was the birthplace of their forefathers. Working forward from that presumption, he argued that the buildings on the sacred soil of Machu Picchu represented a sanctuary, complete with a convent where women chosen from across the Inca empire came to serve the Inca leader and his coterie as 'Virgins of the Sun'. As evidence, he pointed to the hundred skeletons that had been excavated since he first stumbled across the site, of whom three-quarters were female. More recent archaeological studies, however, have shown a fifty-fifty split between male and female bones buried there.

As a sanctuary, the theory runs, Machu Picchu would in its original form have also been a pilgrimage site, which would explain why it was so much smaller than other Inca cities (large enough for just 700 residents), though the challenges of its geography would surely have also played a part in that. Archaeological evidence makes plain that the Inca weren't the only people to live at Machu Picchu. Among the bones that have been found are those of others from coastal regions of modern-day Peru and Chile, as well as from far-flung parts of the Andes. Ceramics typical of those made by communities as far away as Lake Titicaca have also been unearthed.

There are some areas of broad agreement between historians and archaeologists. They mostly concur that the buildings at Machu Picchu date back to around 1450, probably to the reign of the Inca Emperor Pachacuti (1438–71) and his successor Tupac (1472–93). They are largely of one mind, too, that Machu Picchu was abandoned about a century later, roughly coinciding with the arrival of the Spanish in South America, intent on plundering its wealth, defeating its rulers and turning the place into a colony. In dispute, though, is why Machu Picchu was left empty. Was it so that the conquistadors couldn't find it, or because the water supply was too unreliable so high up, or because an outbreak of disease (possibly smallpox) wiped out its inhabitants? Likewise, there are divergent views on the exact purpose that the builders of this collection of palaces and temples, plazas and platforms, dwellings and storehouses had in mind for their creation.

Some say it was one of a series of pre-conquest *pucaras* – fortified sites located in the mountains to enable the Incas to control an empire that spread across both coastal and highland regions of present-day Bolivia, Ecuador, Chile and northern Argentina as well as Peru. Others describe it as a royal retreat, or summer palace, but the favoured explanation remains that it was some sort of religious sanctuary. Beyond the why, though, there is the how – how were the hundreds and possibly thousands of blocks of stone required for the construction transported to such an inaccessible site by a civilization that knew nothing of wheels, and did not possess anything much by way of beasts of burden beyond the llamas that still feed on the grass on its terraces? And, given that the Incas do not appear to have possessed metal tools, how did they shape, polish and fit together so precisely, elegantly and resiliently those stones into buildings that remain for the most part intact, save for their roofs, almost 600 years later? It is, one visitor once remarked, like building the great basilica of Saint Peter's in Rome without being allowed to use any sort of ladder.

✻

Today's Inca Trail – or Camino Inca/Inka, as it is often referred to – carries the more determined among modern tourists through mountain passes and above-the-clouds outcrops of the Amazon rainforest to Machu Picchu (for the faint-hearted, or time-poor, there is a train that does it in three-and-a half hours each way from Cusco to the nearest town to the site, Aguas Calientes). The infrastructure of the trail is largely unchanged, thanks once again to the extraordinary durability of Inca engineering. The tunnels, stone staircases up and down sheer mountain slopes, and high, unbending retaining walls are those that would have carried and protected pilgrims to the sanctuary at Machu Picchu five centuries ago. In 1535, Hernando Pizarro, younger brother of Francisco, who led the Spanish Conquistadors in defeating and subjugating the Inca Empire, was one who left his footprints on other sections of the Inca Trail. 'The path in the mountains', he wrote, 'is something to see because it is built in very difficult terrain. In the Christian world, we have not seen such beautiful roads. All of the crossings have bridges of stone or wood.'[4]

The Incas were, then, skilled, ingenious and industrious folk. Like the Romans, their fellow empire builders, before them, they sought to join their far-flung domains (which they called Tahuant-insuyo – or Four Regions) with a network of stone roadways, 23,000 kilometres in all, known as Qhapaq Ñan. It stretched out across both coastal plains – where the paved thoroughfares were as much as 5 or even 6 metres wide – and the high mountains. Here the terrain demanded that they be narrower, sometimes no more than 1 metre, but these were still vital military, administrative and trading arteries, as well as a route for those who walked them to sacred sites. Quite why the Incas chose to build these pathways in the mountains – there is an easier, flatter route to Machu Picchu that would follow the basin of the river Urubamba (and is used by the railway today) – is another mystery, but it seems to have had something to do with the place that nature, and its gods, played in the culture. Why take the easier option when you could walk with the gods?

As well as being practical, then, the Incas were also profoundly religious. They integrated the worship of the sun god, Inti, whom they regarded as their ancestor, into a seamless theocratic state. Each Inca emperor was part god, part human, while Inti, in human form, featured in public buildings on golden disks from which rays and flames extended. In June, Inti-Raymi took place, one of a cycle of festivals, where the sun god was honoured and placated with animal sacrifices and ritual dances. The Inca pantheon was large, its gods and spirits all found in nature – in the moon, the stars, the mountains, the rivers and forests. The parallels are striking with modern-day Shamanism – or, what academics call Neo-Shamanism, since many of its practices are drawn from, or based, on ancient and indigenous religions – especially in regard to connecting the divine with nature and the earth.

At the starting point for the section of the Inca Trail that leads to Machu Picchu lies the old Inca imperial capital, Cusco, sacked by Francisco Pizarro in 1535. Before that, it is said, the city had been designed in the shape of a puma, a sacred animal to the Inca, but it was substantially rebuilt following the conquest. Some remains of Inca worship are still there – the Emperor's golden palace, the

Qorikancha, also referred to as the Temple of the Sun, as well as a Temple of the Virgins of the Sun, the same all-female group that Bingham believed was based in Machu Picchu. Once visitors set off along the trail itself, there are regular reminders that it too was once (for some travellers at least) a sacred pathway. The ruins of ritual baths can be seen at the settlement of Wiñay Wayna (which translates as 'Forever Young'), on a steep slope overlooking the Urubamba River, while at Patallacta there is a shrine, called Pulpituyuq, with rounded walls where religious ceremonies are believed to have taken place.

The presence of the sacred for Incas who walked this trail, though, would not only have been manifest in what buildings they had constructed alongside it. It was there in the landscape that crowds in on the trail from every side and angle. Each mountain would have its own *apu* – or spirit. Among these, none was greater in the region than that of the snow-tipped Salkantay, 6,250 metres high, the 'Savage Mountain'. Its *apu* was revered as one of the principal deities controlling weather and fertility. Inca gods could be both benign and destructive. The Andes is an earthquake zone (one reason no mortar was used in construction is thought to have been that it left stones free to 'dance' when tremors occurred, without being dislodged), and the goddess Pachamama was regarded as an earth mother, whose good moods would cause crops planted in the mountains to flourish, while her rages – if, for example, sufficient animal and human sacrifice had not been made to her – could cause the ground to convulse and break open. To this day, each August, at the high point of the planting season, local farmers will make offerings on coca leaves to her, though her original Inca personality – as both mother and sometimes wife of the sun god, Inti – has since colonial times been merged in rituals with aspects of Catholic veneration of the Virgin Mary.

One of the most popular itineraries on the Camino Inca towards Machu Picchu starts at Piscacucho, a small village outside Cusco. From there, over four days and three nights, parties of walkers, accompanied by guides and porters, head off on a gruelling climb towards Dead Woman's Pass – Warmiwañusqa – at 4,200 metres, followed by 'Cloud-Level Town' – Phuyupatamarca – at 3,650 metres, before descending over 1,000 metres via a 1,500-step Inca stone staircase towards the Sun Gate or *Intipunku* that Hiram Bingham walked through to catch his first glimpse of Machu Picchu. It is tough going, made harder still by the sickness many experience at high altitude, as well as the constant danger that comes with crossing mountains. Plunging drops are all around should a foot be put in the wrong place, and infrastructure to mitigate the risk is rudimentary. Yet, as discussed, most notably in relation to the Celtic monks and Bardsey Island, putting yourself in peril, as well as sheer endurance, can be part and parcel of the pilgrim experience.

Most of those who walk the Inca Trail time their arrival at the Sun Gate to coincide with sunrise, when the air of magic and mystery about Machu Picchu is at its most potent. When the guards open the gates at 6 a.m., hikers are drawn down into a place that gives every impression of being otherworldly. Indeed, the appeal of experiencing precisely this feeling has become so great that, since 2016, the Peruvian authorities have limited the number of passes it issues to walk the main Inca Trail to just 500 per day, of which more than half usually go to guides and porters.

Those who do not plan well in advance, or prefer not to use one of the accredited tourist companies that can access passes easily, have therefore to seek alternative routes through the mountains to Machu Picchu. Neither the Lares nor the Salkantay routes are restricted, and to add to their charms they are – unlike the Inca

Trail, which one recent American visitor likened to George Washington Bridge over the Hudson in New York at rush hour – generally uncrowded, allowing walkers a greater sense of being 'away from things' and at one with nature, though they are still used by locals carrying bananas and avocados to market. The Lares, though it goes higher, is said to be easier to walk, but the main drawback is it arrives at Machu Picchu not at the Sun Gate, but below the citadel itself, and so requires some mixing with day-trippers.

※

Those academics who study the many manifestations of modern pilgrimages have created a special category for what they label 'power places'. These are sites whose popularity has been on the rise since the 1960s, writes the scholar Michael Stausberg, as locations that 'are often at the same time national tourism icons and sites of archaeological activities and concern, but also pertinent landmarks on the mental and spiritual global map of the New Age, various paganisms, or forms of contemporary religions (Druids, Goddess Movements and the like).'5 Among those he lists are Stonehenge, the Egyptian pyramids, the Taj Mahal, Uluru (Ayers Rock) in Australia, and Sedona (an Arizona desert town surrounded by strange red-rock buttes), as well as both Cusco and Machu Picchu. Just as at other more mainstream, historically verifiable religious sites pilgrims gather for their services and rituals, at these 'power places' a new generation of spiritual travellers come to perform theirs.

In the case of Machu Picchu, these tend to be led by Shaman guides. The citadel itself gives them plenty of scope. Archaeologists have divided the buildings of Machu Picchu into all sorts of groupings to satisfy their own pet theories as to the origins and purpose of the place, but the existence of a sanctuary or ceremonial area, sometimes called Sacred Plaza, cordoned off from the warehouses and residential buildings by walls, ditches and what might be a moat, is widely acknowledged. The major draw in this section for tourists and seekers alike is the carved rock that stands on a pyramid-like terrace. In the Inca belief system, it is speculated, this Intihuatana Stone (a name that in Quecha roughly means 'hitching post of the sun') represented one end of an invisible connection between earth and the sun that is akin to that between a kite and the person on the end of the string.

As part of the stone's base, there is a series of recesses that suggests it may once have been used as some kind of altar in ceremonies. Then there is a curious and unmissable protruding tab that faces magnetic north and, during the rainy season, is reported to point directly to the Southern Cross constellation, long used as a key reference point by navigators. And, at that moment, the Southern Cross is directly over the summit of nearby Salkantay. Meanwhile, at sunrise on the summer solstice in December, the sun's light projects through spaces in and around the Intihuatana Stone to produce a triangular pattern that illuminates two unexplained concentric circles on the floor next to it. Whether this was a sundial, or some kind of calendar measurement, has never been satisfactorily answered.

The same potent mixture of astrology, geography, ceremony and worship of the earth spirits is seen in other parts of Machu Picchu, but the stone is certainly the most striking example. Some historians wonder whether it was its presence in particular, and its reputation, that caused Machu Picchu to be abandoned and mothballed when news of the conquistadors' arrival was first heard. The Incas did not want this sacred object to be looted or damaged. The destruction subsequently wrought on similar structures at other Inca sites that were occupied by the Spanish suggests that such caution was justified.

Other buildings on the site also seem to have been fashioned to capture specific natural effects – like the Room (or Temple) of Three Windows, where a row of giant openings faces out eastwards as if for a purpose. And at the Torreon, or Sun Temple, a rare curved structure in the otherwise neat geometry of lines at Machu Picchu, a beam of light shines through a window on the winter solstice (21 June in the southern hemisphere), forming a mysterious rectangle atop a slab of granite. The Torreon, some suggest, may have been an observatory of sorts, its now missing roof domed. That could have been what inspired the Swiss author Erich von Däniken, in his 1968 best-seller, *Chariots of the Gods?*, to float theories that Machu Picchu's origins had something to do with alien visitors to earth from outer space.

Then there is Intimachay or the 'cave of the sun'. This cavern, situated just below the main ruins, has a single east-facing window. For forty-nine weeks of each year, no light enters via it to illuminate the cave's deepest, darkest recesses. At sunrise during the ten days before and after the summer solstice in December, however, the sun's first rays briefly shine through the window and onto Inti-machay's rear wall. Again, there is a bevy of theories about this. Most revolve around it having been the spot where the Incas would observe the feast of the sun god, possibly including an initiation ritual where young boys would have their ears pierced to mark their journey towards manhood.

None of this can be conclusively proved, but even the most casual visitor, treating Machu Picchu as a mysterious museum in the clouds, will realize it was built to show off to best effect the wonders of nature. That includes not just being perched on top of a mountain itself, but the alignment of its buildings with the surrounding peaks. For modern-day devotees of Shamanism in particular,[6] that has great appeal in their search for 'earth energy centres', which they believe have a particular and intense resonance with each individual's 'chakras'. These are the seven key points, familiar to those who practise yoga, where energy flows in the body. Some are so keen to access these energy centres undisturbed that reports tell of groups trying to slip into Machu Picchu at night, when its gates are locked.

Around Machu Picchu, too, a whole network has developed in recent years to welcome New Age pilgrims hoping that, in the shadow of the mysterious citadel, they will find some sort of epiphany in their lives. Spas, retreat centres and hotels, some of them very expensive, offer Shaman-guided and -led treks and tours of the main site, ritual cleansings, healings and 'payment to earth' ceremonies. Often these are run by, and in conjunction with, the local Quecha-speaking people, whose ancestors would have followed the same nature-orientated belief systems as the Incas, but in more recent generations also imbibed the Catholicism that came with colonialism. The resulting hybrid can be an attractive catch-all, mishmash of traditions, fuelled by drinking locally brewed *ayahuasca*, made from the leaves of plants (some of them collected at early morning religious ceremonies) that have hallucinogenic qualities. Such cocktails were regarded as 'the work of the devil' by Catholic missionaries who arrived with the Spanish, but today it is part of what travellers, tourists and pilgrims alike refer to as a distinctively 'hippy vibe' around Machu Picchu.

It is, though, just one aspect of how this site has developed in the century since Hiram Bingham alerted the world to its existence. Once the Quecha had wanted to keep it hidden from outside eyes. Its opening up in the twentieth century has undeniably brought financial benefits to the area. Yet the crowds who have come have also placed a strain on this historic site, on the local infrastructure and on their way of life. The 'success' of a pilgrimage route can bring mixed blessings, something that applies to all the routes discussed.

TO ARRIVE WHERE WE STARTED

᪥

'If you came this way,
Taking any route, starting from anywhere,
At any time or at any season,
It would always be the same: you would have to put off
Sense and notion. You are not here to verify,
Instruct yourself, or inform curiosity
Or carry report. You are here to kneel
Where prayer has been valid.'

T. S. ELIOT, 'LITTLE GIDDING' (1942)[1]

Journey's end? Not quite. T. S. Eliot is, for me, the poet who best captures pilgrimage in all its many aspects. In 'Little Gidding', the final poem of his *Four Quartets*, he describes how its appeal spans the generations, the centuries, and the faiths. To go on pilgrimage is to join a human chain whose links stretch back through millennia on a journey that takes us – whether religious, spiritual or neither of the above – to where once 'prayer has been valid'. And that fact, even in our secular times, permeates the location in question, and sometimes the road that leads to it, with a distinctive atmosphere.

It was true in 1936 when Eliot went to the church in the remote village of Little Gidding, deep in the flatlands of the east of England, where a high-minded seventeenth-century Anglican community had lived. It is equally true today on the different routes covered in this book, whether visitors chose to drink it in or overlook it.

A certain curiosity about belief does, however, make those on pilgrim paths more receptive, passively or actively, but the act of walking in the footsteps of those who have trodden the same path for hundreds, if not thousands, of years, means that all-comers are potentially open to it. For they are, as Eliot expresses so well, stepping out of one type of time, and into another, longer in its sweep. They certainly don't have to get on their knees, or pray, or light a candle, or even feel drawn to do so. Just being there will expose the modern pilgrim to the sheer accumulation of all that past generations of pilgrims have brought and offered up there – their pains and their joys, their wishes and their fears, their beliefs and their doubts. Such a concentration, laid bare in these locations before some hoped-for greater power, means the gap narrows between the visible, tangible, twenty-first-century, technological and scientifically advanced world and an invisible, ageless, ill-defined, metaphysical and spiritual dimension – if such a thing exists at all. And so, for each pilgrim, the possibility of bridging it is there, too. That continues to exert a pull, even in sceptical times, because the big questions of life, death and suffering that have always confronted human beings, might just be brought into sharp relief.

The list of such pilgrim places has grown down the centuries. While some are known around the globe, other more recent additions appeal to a much smaller audience of seekers. Some have no obvious religious roots and yet attract visitors who, in some important regards, assume the mantle of pilgrims. Like the steady stream of (mainly) young seekers who head into the challenging terrain of central Alaska's remote Denali National Park to an out-of-the-way spot some 50 kilometres from any town. They are walking in the footsteps of Chris McCandless, an American graduate whose own troubled relationship with the world finds an echo in their lives. In the early 1990s, he gave all his belongings to charity and set off into the wilderness to make a new life for himself. His aim wasn't explicitly religious, but such a search for enlightenment was precisely what holy men and women have done down the ages, from the Buddha to the desert fathers of third-century Christianity.

McCandless settled in an abandoned Fairbanks bus that had been left as a makeshift shelter for hunters. He stayed four months and, aged 24, died there. The diaries that he had kept later formed the basis of a hugely popular book about him,[2] and an award-winning film, both entitled *Into the Wild*. The evidence they present suggests strongly that he died as a result of food poisoning, having eaten wild berries or something foraged. Yet for the modern-day pilgrims, the story that he took asceticism to such extremes that he starved himself to death has become a kind of gospel that draws them to the place of his demise. For some, their hankering for communion with the spirit of McCandless is such that they make a ritual of sleeping in the bus where he died, just as medieval pilgrims would spend the night before the relics of a chosen saint in the place where he or she had ended their life on earth.

McCandless's overwhelming desire to seek seclusion in such an unlikely cell in the back of beyond may seem odd to many, but it would have made perfect sense to one of the twentieth century's most fêted writers, the traveller Patrick Leigh Fermor. In the 1950s, he lived for a period in several remote monasteries and reflected that in their silence, separateness and repeated routine, 'the troubled waters of the mind grow still and clear, and much that is hidden away and all that clouds it floats to the surface can be skimmed away; and after a time one reaches a state of peace that is unthought of in the ordinary world.'[3]

The trail to the wilds of Alaska reveals another facet of modern pilgrimage – the need it serves for going back to the original or the source. Just as art lovers, despite the ready availability of lavishly illustrated books, or high-quality prints of great paintings, feel compelled to journey to see the canvas in the raw, in whichever museum that displays it, so too does the modern pilgrim want to see and experience for themselves those places which lay some claim to allowing a particularly acute insight into the human condition.

It is a quality that makes an at-first-glance unlikely link between a rusting bus in Alaska and the pristine, well-ordered war cemeteries of northern France and beyond. They, too, attract a growing number of visitors who show some of the traits of pilgrims. The English author and poet Rudyard Kipling visited these graveyards almost a century ago to remember his son, John, who like the hundreds of thousands buried here, had been killed in the trenches of the First World War. He described the scene that greeted him as a 'Dead Sea of arrested lives'. In the uniform design for all Commonwealth War Graves Commission graveyards, both in France, and those later established around the world to remember those who died in the Second World War and subsequent conflicts, the language and paraphernalia of religion are missing by design. There are no crosses or angels rising from the row after row of identical, rectangular, off-white gravestones. Each does include in its engraving a religious symbol, but the order in which they are arranged is not related to professed belief, rank or, necessarily, date. And as the focal point of each graveyard, Edwin Lutyens's Stone of Remembrance and Reginald Blomfield's Sword of Sacrifice, are specifically not an altar and crucifix (though they might be taken as such by those with eyes to see them thus).

The assumption of faith, which elsewhere is the bedrock of pilgrim sites around the globe as well as the traditional fall-back in the face of such incomprehensible human tragedy as afflicted so many in the two world wars, was deliberately kept at bay in these cemeteries. Yet, as the book of remembrance in each well-tended graveyard ably demonstrates, they have been attracting a growing number of visitors in recent decades who are more pilgrims than mourners. Once, it would have been the immediate relatives of those who were buried there who came, often on trips arranged and funded by the commission. Later, it was their descendants, intent on exploring the family history. Their numbers have thinned with time but now there is another group – those who want to walk in the footsteps of those who died that we might live, to have the chance not just to remember the dead, but also to reflect – as at pilgrim shrines – on the true meaning of their lives and life itself in places so overwhelmingly full of death.

Some of these cemeteries have over the years been part of my own pilgrimages, sitting in my memory alongside trips to the traditional religious destinations of the Catholic upbringing that I wrote of at the start of this book. Here, at the end, though, it feels right to reflect on another pilgrimage more in the flexible twenty-first-century spirit of the word, taken in 2019 with a group to El Salvador.[4] Its focus was not so much on a place as in the past, but on a person, Oscar Romero. He was an outspoken Catholic Archbishop of San Salvador from 1977 to 1980, hailed in his life as 'the voice of the voiceless' for defending the poor and marginalized during his country's collapse into civil war.

It cost him dearly. He was assassinated by those who wished to silence him, and is regarded as a hero and role model by many. In

2018, the Church declared him a saint. So the group I joined was walking, as pilgrims have done for centuries, in the footsteps of one whose belief in God was unwavering, to stand in the places where he stood, and touch the things he left behind in the hope that they would leave some indelible mark on our lives.

That much was deeply traditional, as was the long-forgotten (and strangely reassuring) ritual of daily mass. But this pilgrimage was simultaneously thoroughly modern because it embraced a whole range of other ambitions: from the socio-political aim of investigating how Romero's legacy continues to influence daily life in what remains a divided and unstable society, to unabashed tourism in a little-known but beautiful landscape of mountains and ocean.

In other words, we were walking with not one but two purposes, the first faith-based and the second secular. They coincided – for me at least – with remarkable ease. The connection was seamless between attending a mass that celebrated the memory of Oscar Romero in a rural community, and then moving next door to hear about that village's efforts to be better farmers by using eco-friendly methods. Some of my more devout co-believers might see such a combination as a step too far in politicizing pilgrimage (a previous Pope, John Paul II, blocked Romero's sainthood for much the same reasons) but for me it showed how and why pilgrimage has remained so relevant even when denominational attachment (in El Salvador as in the West) is tumbling.

What took me most by surprise, though – because it hadn't figured much, if at all, in my initial decision to sign up – was the gift of the companionship of a group of thirty like(ish)-minded strangers. If Chaucer's pilgrims on the road to Canterbury bonded in a way that went beyond their shared, ostensibly religious excursion, then the same was true in our case (though perhaps not quite so uproariously), despite all of us being drawn from much more individualistic me-me-me societies. It was there in the shared meals, in the shared concern for the welfare of a group that ranged widely in physical stamina and in age from 18 to 80, and most of all in the gradual emergence amid the general slowness that remains a hallmark of pilgrimage, of each individual's back-home-back-story and why they were there. These are things that no longer always happen readily or easily in our fragmented communities, where the emphasis has swung towards looking after what is yours, being suspicious of the stranger, and sticking to your own backyard.

Their presence on this trip, and on others from the Camino to Shikoku, is one more factor in the renaissance of pilgrimage in otherwise atomized times. The same sort of instant bonding, it is true, can be seen in the friendships that spring up in double-quick time on holidays, but the shared aspect of searching for meaning that is implicit in the word pilgrimage makes it more intense and enduring. A pilgrimage isn't, then, just another word for holiday. It is more than taking a break from everyday life to recharge your batteries and relax. What pilgrimage is about, however circuitously, is taking a longer, slower, and hence more profound look at life, and doing it in a way that modern existence finds hard to accommodate – by stopping, pausing and reflecting, usually in the company of others, living and dead.

> *With the drawing of this Love and the voice of this Calling*
> *We shall not cease from exploration*
> *And the end of all our exploring*
> *Will be to arrive where we started*
> *And know the place for the first time*

T. S. Eliot, 'Little Gidding'[5]

NOTES

Introduction

1 Alan Bennett, 'Allelujah', extracts from his 2018 diary, *London Review of Books* (3 January 2019).
2 Bess Twiston Davies, 'Oh to be a pilgrim in Britain's green and pleasant land', *The Times*, 21 September 2019.
3 In the English lyric poet's 1867 eulogy to the decline of religion, 'Dover Beach'.
4 Rebecca Solnit, *Wanderlust: A History of Walking* (London: Verso, 2001).
5 Gerard W. Hughes, *Walk to Jerusalem: In Search of Peace* (London: Darton, Longman & Todd, 1991).

1 Santiago de Compostela

1 Quoted in Peter Davies, *Leading Matters: How to Enjoy and Lead a Walk in Ten Easy Steps* (London: Grosvenor House Publishing, 2014).
2 Nancy Louise Frey, *Pilgrim Stories: On and Off the Road to Santiago* (Berkeley: University of California Press, 1998).
3 https://galiwonders.com/en/blog/camino-santiago-2017-statistics/
4 Ibid.
5 Ibid.
6 By the distinguished British lawyer Jonathan Sumption in *Pilgrimage: An Image of Medieval Religion* (London: Faber and Faber, 1975).
7 Jonathan Sumption, *Pilgrimage: An Image of Medieval Religion* (London: Faber and Faber, 1975).

8 He is also reputed to have brought the Holy Grail, the cup used by Jesus at the Last Supper, and its connection with Glastonbury subsequently played a part in the Arthurian legend.
9 From a private copy of the unpublished journal, shared with the author.

2 Jerusalem

1 Translated by B. A. Windeatt, *The Book of Margery Kempe* (London: Penguin Books, 1985).
2 Ibid.
3 Surah 17:1, *The Qur'an*, trans. by M. A. S. Abdel Haleem (Oxford: OUP, 2010).
4 Venerable Bede, *Ecclesiastical History of the English People*, ed. D. H. Farmer (London: Penguin, 2003).
5 Ibid.
6 Gerard W. Hughes, *In Search of a Way* (London: Darton, Longman & Todd, 1986) and *Walk to Jerusalem: In Search of Peace* (London: Darton, Longman & Todd, 1991).
7 Guy Stagg, *The Crossway* (London: Picador, 2018).
8 Ibid.

3 Rome

1 As recalled in one of his famous 'Table Talks' (number 6059) to his followers.
2 Ibid. (number 3428).
3 *The Path to Rome* is today available online at https://www.gutenberg.org/files/7373/7373-h/7373-h.htm

4 Figures provided by the Confraternity of Pilgrims to Rome.

5 According to figures quoted in Cicerone Guides.

6 Brian Mooney, *A Long Way for a Pizza: On Foot to Rome* (London: Thorogood, 2012).

7 Christopher Lambert, *Taking a Line for a Walk* (Woodbridge: Antique Collectors' Club, 2004).

8 Matthew 16:18, *The Jerusalem Bible*, popular edition (London: Darton, Longman & Todd, 1974).

9 Early evidence for the tradition is found in the *Letter to the Romans* by Saint Ignatius, the early second-century Bishop of Antioch. It is probable that the tradition of a twenty-five-year episcopate of Peter in Rome began not earlier than the beginning or the middle of the third century.

10 From *Julius Exclusus* (1517) in J. A. Froude, *Life and Letters of Erasmus* (London, 1895).

11 John 10:9, *The Jerusalem Bible*, popular edition (London: Darton, Longman & Todd, 1974).

12 Judith Champ, *The English Pilgrimage to Rome* (Leominster: Gracewing, 2000).

13 Edited E. Parthey, *Mirabilia Urbis Romae* (Rome: Berolini, 1869).

14 Lynne Withey, *Grand Tours and Cook's Tours: A History of Leisure Travel 1750 to 1915* (New York: William Morrow, 1997).

15 Ibid.

4 Mecca

1 Sir Richard Burton, *Personal Narrative of a Pilgrimage to Al-Madinah and Meccah* (London: Tylston and Edwards, 1893).

2 Ibid.

3 Ibid.

4 Ibid.

5 Jason Mohammad, *Y Daith* on the TV channel S4C, 8 November 2009.

6 Surah 22:27, *The Qur'an*, trans. by M. A. S. Abdel Haleem (Oxford: OUP, 2010).

7 *The Autobiography of Malcolm X* (New York: Grove Press, 1965).

8 Muhammad ibn Ishaq, *Sirat Rasul Allah*, 969, translated by A. Guillaume, *The Life of Muhammad* (Oxford: OUP, 1955).

9 Genesis, Chapters 16 and 21, *The Jerusalem Bible*, popular edition (London: Darton, Longman & Todd, 1974).

10 Surah 2:124–127, *The Qur'an*, trans. by M. A. S. Abdel Haleem (Oxford: OUP, 2010).

6 Lourdes, Medjugorje and the Marian Shrines

1 Victor Turner and Edith Turner, *Image and Pilgrimage in Christian Culture* (New York: Columbia University Press, 1978).

2 Jean-Pierre Bely, speaking in the BBC Radio 4 programme, *The Miracle Men*, broadcast on 11 January 2002.

3 In an interview for this book with the author.

4 Colm Tóibín, *The Sign of the Cross: Travels in Catholic Europe* (London: Jonathan Cape, 1994).

5 Gerard W. Hughes, *Walk to Jerusalem: In Search of Peace* (London: Darton, Longman & Todd, 1991).

6 James Mulligan, *Medjugorje: What's Happening?* (Brewster, Mass: Paraclete Press, 2011).

7 Desmond Seward, *The Dancing Sun: Journeys to the Miracle Shrines* (London: Macmillan, 1993).

8 James Mulligan, *Medjugorje: What's Happening* (Brewster, Mass: Paraclete Press, 2008).

7 The North Wales Pilgrim's Way

1 In the collection *Frequencies* (London: Macmillan, 1978).

2 The tenth-century text, *Brendan's Voyage*, of which over 100 manuscripts exist throughout Europe.

3 See Ian Bradley, *Celtic Christianity: Making Myths and Chasing Dreams* (Edinburgh: Edinburgh University Press, 1999).

4 John O'Donohue, *Anam Cara: A Book of Celtic Wisdom* (London: Bantam, 1996).

5 The British Library has a digitized version of his *Itinerarium Cambriae*.

6 See Victor Turner and Edith Turner, *Image and Pilgrimage in Christian Culture* (New York: Columbia University Press, 1978).

7 Peter Stanford, *The Extra Mile* (London: Continuum, 2012).

8 A popular choice is: compiled by Jim Cotter, *Etched by Silence: A Pilgrimage Through the Poetry of R. S. Thomas* (Norwich: Canterbury Press, 2013).

9 In the collection *Frequencies* (London: Macmillan, 1978).

8 Kumbh Mela

1 Referenced in his article, 'Kumbh Mela Festival', on the BBC News website, 11 January 2012.

2 See Kama Maclean, *Pilgrimage and Power: The Kumbh Mela in Allahabad, 1765–1954* (Oxford: OUP, 2008).

9 The Buddha Trail

1 In 'The Buddhist Trail', *Condé Nast Traveller* (12 September 2012).

2 Henry Clarke Warren, *Buddhism in Translation* (Cambridge, Mass: Harvard University Press, 1896).

3 Edwin Arnold, *The Light of Asia: Being the Life and Teaching of Gautama, Prince of India and Founder of Buddhism* (London: Trübner & Co., 1879).

4 Karen Armstrong, *Buddha* (London: Weidenfeld & Nicolson, 2000).

5 From Kosho Yamanoto's version of the *Nibbana Sutta*, translated by Dr Tony Page in 2004.

6 Stephen Batchelor, *Confessions of a Buddhist Atheist* (New York: Spiegel & Grau, 2010).

10 Shikoku

1 Figures provided by Robert Sibley, *The Way of the 88 Temples* (Charlottesville: University of Virginia Press, 2013).

2 See research from the Ehime University Research Center for the Shikoku Henro and Pilgrimages of the World.

3 English translation from Oliver Statler, *Japanese Pilgrimage* (London: Pan, 1984).

11 North America

1 In multiple formats online at Project Gutenberg.

2 *Peace Pilgrim: Her Life and Work in Her Own Words* (New Mexico: Ocean Tree, 1982).

3 Ibid.

4 Ibid.

5 Ibid.

6 Rebecca Solnit, *Wanderlust: A History of Walking* (London: Verso, 2001).

12 Machu Picchu

1 Describing his book *The Tao of Travel: Enlightenments from Lives on the Road* in 2011 (New York: Houghton Mifflin Harcourt, 2011).

2 Hiram Bingham, *Lost City of the Incas* (London: Weidenfeld & Nicolson, 2003).

3 See the website of the bestselling British writer Graham Hancock: grahamhancock.com.

4 Pedro de Cieza de León, *The Discovery and Conquest of Peru: Chronicles of the New World Encounter* (Durham, NC: Duke University Press, 1998).

5 Michael Stausberg, *Religion and Tourism: Crossroads, Destinations and Encounters* (London: Routledge, 2011).

6 There are no reliable statistics to estimate their number, but in the UK Census in 2011 80,000 people chose pagan to describe themselves from a list of religious affiliations (in which shamanism wasn't offered).

Epilogue

1 T. S. Eliot, *Little Gidding* (London: Faber and Faber, 1942).

2 Jon Krakauer, *Into the Wild* (New York: Random House, 1996).

3 Patrick Leigh Fermor, *A Time to Keep Silence* (London: Queen Anne Press, 1957).

4 Organized by the Romero Trust, a London-based charity (romerotrust.org.uk).

5 T. S. Eliot, *Little Gidding* (London: Faber and Faber, 1942).

FURTHER READING

General

Mick Brown, *The Spiritual Tourist: A Personal Odyssey Through the Outer Reaches of Belief*, London: Bloomsbury, 1998

Geoffrey Chaucer, *The Canterbury Tales*, London: Penguin Books, 2005

T. S. Eliot, *Little Gidding*, London: Faber and Faber, 1942

The Book of Margery Kempe, trans. B. A. Windeatt, London: Penguin Books, 1985

Jon Krakauer, *Into the Wild*, New York: Random House, 1996

Patrick Leigh Fermor, *A Time to Keep Silence*, London: Queen Anne Press, 1957

Matthew Neale, *Pilgrims* [a novel], London: Atlantic Books, 2020

Michael Stausberg, *Religion and Tourism: Crossroads, Destinations and Encounters*, London: Routledge, 2011

Jonathan Sumption, *Pilgrimage: An Image of Medieval Religion*, London: Faber and Faber, 1975

Santiago de Compostela

Paulo Coelho, *The Pilgrimage*, London: HarperCollins, 1995

Nancy Frey, *Pilgrim Stories: On and Off the Road to Santiago*, Berkeley: University of California Press, 1998

Hape Kerkeling, *I'm Off Then: Losing and Finding Myself on the Camino de Santiago*, trans. Shelley Frisch, London: Simon & Schuster, 2017

Shirley MacLaine, *The Camino: A Journey of the Spirit*, London: Simon & Schuster, 2000

Jerusalem

Karen Armstrong, *A History of Jerusalem: One City, Three Faiths*, London: HarperCollins, 1996

Justin Butcher, *Walking to Jerusalem: Blisters, Hope and Other Facts on the Ground*, London: Hodder & Stoughton, 2018

Gerard W. Hughes, *Walk to Jerusalem: In Search of Peace*, London: Darton, Longman & Todd, 1991

Simon Sebag Montefiore, *Jerusalem: The Biography*, London: Phoenix, 2011

Guy Stagg, *The Crossway*, London: Picador, 2018

Rome

Hilaire Belloc, *The Path to Rome* (1902), www.gutenberg.org

Judith Champ, *The English Pilgrimage to Rome*, Leominster: Gracewing, 2000

Gerard W. Hughes, *In Search of a Way*, London: Darton, Longman & Todd, 1986

Christopher Lambert, *Taking a Line for a Walk*, Woodbridge: Antique Collectors' Club, 2004

Brian Mooney, *A Long Way for a Pizza: On Foot to Rome*, London: Thorogood, 2012

Mecca

Irfan Ali Beg, *A Pilgrimage to Mecca* (1896), Norderstedt: Hansebooks, 2019

Karen Armstrong, *Islam: A Short History*, London: Weidenfeld & Nicolson, 2011

Sir Richard Burton, *Personal Narrative
of a Pilgrimage to Al-Madinah and
Meccah*, 2 vols, London: Tylston
and Edwards, 1893
Idries Shah, *Destination Mecca* (1957),
London: ISF Publishing, 2019

Lalibela
John Binns, *The Orthodox Church of
Ethiopia: A History*, London: I. B.
Tauris, 2017
Cristina García Rodero, *Lalibela*,
Madrid: La Fabrica, 2017
Jacques Mercier and Claude Lepage,
Lalibela: Wonder of Ethiopia,
London: Paul Holberton
Publishing, 2011

Marian Shrines
Mary Craig, *Spark from Heaven:
The Mystery of the Madonna of
Medjugorje*, Notre Dame, Indiana:
Ave Maria Press, 1988
James Mulligan, *Medjugorje: What's
Happening?*, Brewster, Mass:
Paraclete Press, 2011
Desmond Seward, *The Dancing Sun:
Journeys to the Miracle Shrines*,
London: Macmillan, 1993
Colm Tóibín, *The Sign of the Cross:
Travels in Catholic Europe*, London:
Jonathan Cape, 1994
Victor Turner and Edith Turner,
*Image and Pilgrimage in Christian
Culture*, New York: Columbia
University Press, 1978

The North Wales Pilgrim's Way
Ian Bradley, *Celtic Christianity: Making
Myths and Chasing Dreams*,
Edinburgh: Edinburgh University
Press, 1999
John O'Donohue, *Anam Cara: A Book
of Celtic Wisdom*, London: Bantam,
1996

Martin Palmer and Nigel Palmer,
*Sacred Britain: A Guide to the
Sacred Sites and Pilgrim Routes
of England, Scotland and Wales*,
London: Piatkus, 1997
Jim Cotter, *Etched by Silence: A
Pilgrimage Through the Poetry of
R. S. Thomas*, Norwich: Canterbury
Press, 2013

Kumbh Mela
Kama Maclean, *Pilgrimage and Power:
The Kumbh Mela in Allahabad,
1765–1954*, Oxford: OUP, 2008
Rahul Mehrotra, *Kumbh Mela:
Mapping the Ephemeral Megacity*,
Delhi: Niyogi Books, 2017
Mark Tully, *The Kumbh Mela*, Varanasi:
Indica Books, 2002

The Buddha Trail
Karen Armstrong, *Buddha*, London:
Weidenfeld & Nicolson, 2000
Edwin Arnold, *The Light of Asia: Being
the Life and Teaching of Gautama,
Prince of India and Founder of
Buddhism*, London: Trübner & Co.,
1879
Henry Clarke Warren, *Buddhism in
Translation*, Cambridge, Mass:
Harvard University Press, 1896

Shikoku
Robert C. Sibley, *The Way of the 88
Temples: Journeys on the Shikoku
Pilgrimage*, Charlottesville:
University of Virginia Press, 2013
Oliver Statler, *Japanese Pilgrimage*,
London: Pan, 1984

North America
*Peace Pilgrim: Her Life and Work in Her
Own Words*, New Mexico: Ocean
Tree, 1982

Rebecca Solnit, *Wanderlust: A History of Walking*, London: Verso, 2001

Machu Picchu
Hiram Bingham, *Lost City of the Incas*, London: Weidenfeld & Nicolson, 2003

Pedro de Cieza de Léon, *The Discovery and Conquest of Peru: Chronicles of the New World Encounter*, Durham, NC: Duke University Press, 1998

Paul Theroux, *The Tao of Travel: Enlightenments from Lives on the Road*, New York: Houghton Mifflin Harcourt, 2011

ACKNOWLEDGMENTS

To cross the world on pilgrimage requires a good support network and I am grateful for the companionship on the route offered by: Remona Aly, Michael Arditti, Twiggy Bigwood, Rachel Billington, Dustin Lance Black, Anthony Coles, Sue Cramp, Clare Dixon, the Reverend Dr Peter Doll, Julian Filochowski, Fiona Fraser, Louis Jebb, Etta Levi-Smythe, Jane Nicholson, Nigel Planer, Guy Stagg, Marina Warner and Martin and Ann Weiler.

It also helps to have plenty of back-up, so my thanks go to Piers Blofeld, my agent, and to Ben Hayes, Isabella Luta and Julia MacKenzie at Thames & Hudson.

And to do it with your family is the best of all worlds, in this, as in everything – to Kit and Orla Stanford, and to Siobhan Cross.

PICTURE CREDITS

INDEX